100
BEST KEPT SECRETS OF

Missouri

Ann M. Hazelwood

100 BEST KEPT SECRETS OF *Missouri*

Virginia Publishing Company
P.O. Box 4538
St. Louis, MO 63108
(314) 367-6612
www.STL-books.com
Please check out our Web site for other books on St. Louis history.

Cover Design by Kate Huffman
Inside Layout Design by Ben Pierce
Copy editors: Fran Levy and MJ McNeece

TABLE OF CONTENTS

Dear Readers,

While you will not be surprised that the State of Missouri is a wonderful place to live, work and raise a family, you may be pleasantly surprised at how many cultural and historic attractions we have that you have yet to enjoy.

From the historic Pony Express in the West, to the modern architecture of the Laumeier Sculpture Park in the East, Missouri has something to offer anyone and everyone in search of adventure.

Please take the time to explore the rich heritage and culture that makes the State of Missouri such a great place.

Sincerely,

MATT BLUNT

Dedication

This book is dedicated to the citizens of Missouri who have become entrepreneurs, farmers, conservationists, artists and public officials for this great state. We have all benefited from your contributions.

I personally want to thank Governor Matt Blunt for his kind words for this book, and to all the contributors who took time to share their "secrets."

I shall always be grateful for the love and encouragement supplied by my husband, Keith Hazelwood, and my sons, Joel and Jason Watkins.

Last, but not least, much appreciation goes to Jeff Fister of Virginia Publishing for giving local authors a chance to write about their topics of interest.

100 BEST KEPT SECRETS OF *Missouri*

Introduction

Missouri is a wonderful state with much diversity and beauty. The state itself is a "secret" that most United States citizens are not aware of. Missourians are quite good about patting themselves on the back within the region but are conservative to the point of keeping their pride close to home. We neglect to brag to the east, west, south and north that we are the heart and soul of this great nation.

Missouri has five regions that offer something for everyone. As I travel this great state, I am impressed and amused with what citizens feel are the best attractions and secrets. I have been amazed at the unique places, historical facts and interesting people that I have met while writing this book.

The "secret" submitters love Missouri and were proud to share information about everything from festivals to incredible caves. You'll find that the secrets are enticing as they whet your appetite for more. They may be locations or statistical information of which Missourians should be proud to boast.

I hope you will become educated, amused, curious and energized to experience all 100 secrets of this "Show Me" state. It gives me a great deal of pleasure to share these secrets with you, and I hope that you pass them on to your family, neighbors and friends.

ANN M. HAZELWOOD

1. The Secret of the Jamesport Amish

Because Jamesport, Missouri, is the largest Amish settlement of the "Old Order" west of the Mississippi River, it is quite the popular tourist attraction in the northwest of our state.

Most come to purchase wholesale produce at their auction three times a week and visit their Amish stores and festivals. It is always a quaint experience.

The secret of this Amish community, however, is the tremendous worldwide industry they have created. There are three sawmills that make pallets for shipping internationally. They also produce Amish-made furniture and supply handmade buggies for other communities. A new facility has been constructed for horse milking: once extracted, the milk is freeze dried and sent to California for use in the manufacture of cosmetics. These are secrets that should be told.

The city of Jamesport is quite proud of the Amish people's success in adding to the economy.

You can visit the active Amish on most days. However, they close their businesses on Thursdays, Sundays, Good Friday, Jan. 6 and Ascension Day.

Submitted by Linda Woodward, Jamesport, Missouri

2. The Secret of the Mother's Shrine

You'll find the "Mother's Shrine" in the National Shrine of St. Mary in Laurie, Missouri. It is one of only 16 shrines in the United States.

The somewhat secret main attraction is the Mother's Wall of Life.

Names of mothers throughout the world are engraved on the polished granite for all to see and feel. Thirty-seven states and 13 countries are represented.

A 14-foot sculpture of Mary stands in the middle of the beautiful fountain and waterfall. Each spring, 25,000 flowers are planted around it. At Christmas, these flowers are replaced with thousands of lights.

Another amazing feature for all to see is the Avenue of Flags. These are flags received from guests from 101 different countries who have visited the shrine.

Get a glimpse of this shrine at www.mothershrine.org.

Submitted by Rose Vanderbeck, Laurie, Missouri

3. The Secret of the Historic Speech at Fulton, Missouri

Located on the campus of Westminster College in Fulton, Missouri, is the beautiful site of the Church of St. Mary the Virgin Aldermanbury, designed by the famous architect Sir Christopher Wren.

It is amazing to know that this church was once in London, England, and brought to this location stone by stone. Beneath the church are the library and museum dedicated to Winston Churchill and a gift shop that offers many items related to Churchill's long career.

In 1946, Churchill was invited to give a brief, inspirational message at the college, where he unexpectedly delivered a major foreign policy statement known as the "Iron Curtain Speech." This in essence began the Cold War, which lasted another 40 years.

Another special attraction, featuring a portion of the Berlin Wall, is a sculpture by Churchill's granddaughter, artist Edwina Sandys.

This incredible piece of history is known worldwide but is a secret in our own midst.

Submitted by Lori J. Dillion, Fulton, Missouri

4. The Secret of the Hunter-Dawson Home Historic Site

This 1859 plantation was used as General Pope's headquarters during the Civil War.

Not generally known is the belief that the plantation is haunted, and a visitor to the site has caught the spirit's image on film. The image appears to be that of a woman's silhouette appearing at the window at night, as well as during the day. Visitors have heard sounds of heavy furniture moving about, heels clicking on the wooden floor, and a piano that strikes its own chord. Puffs of air frequently are blown into visitors' ears. Do not let the mysterious and eerie communication keep you from visiting this beautiful, historic structure.

This historical home is located on the huge Mississippi River bend in New Madrid, Missouri. The great earthquakes of 1811 and 1812 created the river bend, believed to be the widest portion of the Mississippi.

History is certainly alive and well in this plantation on the river's edge.

Submitted by Margaret Palmer, New Madrid, Missouri

5. The Secret of the Elms Resort and Spa

Since 1888, the Elms Hotel in Excelsior Springs, Missouri, has been entertaining guests, who enjoy the historic charm and the services of a contemporary four-star hotel.

Challenges have been significant throughout the years, with a fire in 1898 and another two years later.

Famous guests such as Al Capone frequented the hotel during the Depression years. On election night in 1948, Harry S. Truman sought refuge at the hotel when he thought he was losing his bid to be re-elected to the Presidency. In the wee hours of the morning, he was awakened with the news that he had won the election. He was quickly rushed away to Kansas City.

Unwanted "haunted guests" are plentiful, such as the mobster who was killed in the hotel, and the maiden in 1900s uniform dress who supervised the housekeeping staff.

"Christmas at the Elms" is like no other. The lobby displays a 15-foot Christmas tree, and the abundance of white twinkling lights in the snow is like a scene out of the movie "It's a Wonderful Life."

Modern-day amenities are abundant at the hotel, such as the hot-stone massages and lovely specialty shops. The Elms is just 30 minutes north of Kansas City, at 401 Regent Street. Call 816-629-2547 for reservations or check out the Web site at www.elmsresort.com.

Submitted by Debbie and Carl Bearden, St. Charles, Missouri

6. The Secret of the Caves in Perry County

Miles and miles of underground adventure are under the earth's crust in Perry County. There are more caves in this county than any other in the state, 650 caves to be sure!

It is a beautiful county of rolling hills, springs, sinkholes and tunnels.

There are three major cave systems in the county. Crevice, the largest, is 28 miles long. Mystery and Moore are the other two, and they each are approximately 16 miles long.

Many types of life inhabit the caves and their waters, such as crayfish and salamanders. The secret to these caves is the tiny fish, found ONLY in Perry County, called the Grotto Sculpin. It is a fish that evolved over thousands of years from the Bandit Sculpin fish, found only in caves.

The openings of these caves are kept secret because they are on private property.

Submitted by Louis Meyer, Perryville, Missouri

7. The Secret of Norborne, Missouri

When traveling through Carroll County, you'll want to seek out Norborne, Missouri. The population is only about 500, and everyone in town knows about The Hammer Museum. Glen Albrecht, approaching his 90th year, has dazzled hardware collectors from around the world with his collection of hammers and related tools.

More than 12,000 pieces are displayed in his museum, which he built near his home. His favorites are the brass goat hammer and the wraparound head hammer. Mr. Albrecht explains that the more unusual the piece, the more he likes it.

You may have seen him on some of the earlier "Antique Road Show" programs, but he now has more hammers than ever before, as he continues to collect.

To make the most of a visit to Norborne, you may want to visit during the Soybean Festival. On Soybean Festival Day the Lions Club has a big parade where the Soybean King appears out of a big soybean on a float. There are beer gardens, contests, and many class reunions during the festival. The local Lions Club has organized the weekend activities for 25 years.

Be sure to call first before dropping in on the Hammer Museum. It's on the west side of town, at 405 Elmwood Street. Call 636-593-3455.

Submitted by Dennis Albrecht, Norborne, Missouri

8. *The Secret of the Crane's Museum*

From Interstate 70 you'll want to pull off at the Williamsburg exit, Exit 161, between St. Louis and Kansas City, to take a trip into the past. No need to look for a parking lot; you can pull your car right up to the front of the Crane's Museum and Marlene's Restaurant.

When you enter this fourth-generation venture, you are greeted by pleasant folks who are happy to take your $5.00 admission fee for the museum or serve you a home-cooked meal.

The museum, at the rear of the building, houses an incredible collection of furniture, toys, barbershop memorabilia, schoolhouse fixtures, quilts, photos, dolls, tools and whatever else one can imagine from the past.

Joe Crane or his staff give personal tours. Joe is especially happy to show off his stone-carved crane, which he purchased at an auction. Two rooms adjacent to the restaurant sell very reasonably priced crafts and antiques.

Next door is the original Crane's Country Store, where unique farm and hunting supplies can be found. You can chat with the locals around the potbelly stove or order one of Crane's bargain sandwiches. "ONE MEAT, ONE CHEESE, ONE DOLLAR" is the sign posted for customers.

This great stop is a visit like no other! Phone toll free at 877-254-3356 or visit the Web site at www.cranesmuseum.com

Submitted by Dave Klostermier, St. Charles, Missouri

9. The Secret of Missouri State Hwy. 100

If you want to experience the best sample of Missouri travel, check out Hwy. 100, which follows the Missouri River. The scenic drive is heavy with white sycamore trees that are spectacular to see in the fall.

Highway 100 begins at 4th Street in downtown St. Louis and ends at Linn, Missouri. The route takes many twists and turns through historic towns where one can enjoy Missouri's Rhineland at its best. Communities such as Gray Summit, Washington, New Haven and Hermann, the wineries and vast opportunities for antiquing lend themselves to the route's ambience.

Most of Missouri Hwy. 100 is part of the Lewis and Clark Trail, which is an added bonus. One section is from Kirkwood Blvd. to 3 miles west of Wildwood. Then the trail turns off on Route T until it ends. Pick it up again northwest of I-44 and continue to 5 miles north of Linn. That is where the trail turns off to Route C.

In approximately 111 miles, one can have a good eyeful and feel of Missouri. For more information on scenic drives, contact the Missouri Division of Tourism at 573-751-4133.

Submitted Anonymously

10. The Secret of Missouri Town 1855

It was a good year in 1855. At least the folks in Lee's Summit, Missouri, thought so. To re-create that year, in 1965 they took 30 sloping acres of green space and developed what is now a living history community.

With original buildings in their reach dating from 1821 to 1860, they formed a master plan to create "Missouri Town 1855." The architecture of twenty-five buildings ranges from a settler's cabin to an antebellum home. A tavern, schoolhouse and church are just some of the typical representations any town would have. The buildings come alive with 1855 activities and authentically dressed workers and craftsmen.

The town has been the setting for several movies, such as "Ride With the Devil," and the television version of "Friendly Persuasion."

The famous Dalton Gang chose to stay at the settlers' cabin in the 1870s. The Adams House, now the Visitors Center, was once a hospital in the Civil War. Professional living-history interpreters cannot wait to tell you more!

Missouri Town 1855 is on the east side of Lake Jacomo in Fleming Park near Blue Springs, Missouri. Call 816-503-4860 for more information.

Submitted by Gordon Julich, Lee's Summit, Missouri

11. The Secret of Ste. Genevieve, Missouri

One of the oldest settlements on the west bank of the Mississippi River is Ste. Genevieve, where many early nineteenth-century restored buildings grace the narrow streets for your enjoyment. The true gem that exemplifies its history, however, is the Church of Ste. Genevieve, often overlooked as such.

Founded in 1752, this much-needed parish started as a vertical-log church near the river. It moved to its current site at 49 Dubourg Place in 1794. In 1837, that church was replaced by a stone church, on which the structure stands today. In 1874, in an editorial in the *Ste. Genevieve Fair Play,* the editor quoted "Let us add to it a steeple that will forever tower and rise toward heaven, and a cross upon its summit that will overlook everything also made by the hands of men of our town, and shine with approbation to the surrounding country." A 14-foot cross then was put atop the steeple on November 1st of 1879.

Its historical beauty is open and free to visitors. Call 573- 883- 2731 if you wish to request a tour.

Ste. Genevieve's Historic Memorial Cemetery is where you'll find the "resting" founders of this church, dating from the 1780s. Because the cemetery was quite damaged from the flood of 1785, there are only 275 surviving tombstones, but 4000-5000 people are believed to be buried there. This solemn visit makes for great appreciation for this unique community.

Submitted by Deanna Kreitler, Ste. Genevieve, Missouri

12. The Secret of "The City of Fountains"

One of the more beautiful secrets of Kansas City, Missouri, is the many fountains that have developed over the past century. The earlier fountains were utilitarian, but now they reflect the beauty and culture of Kansas City.

In 1973, Harold and Peggy Rue and the Parks and Recreation Department decided that this would enhance tourism and encouraged all future developments to incorporate fountains into their plans.

Rome, Italy, is the only city in the world with more fountains. Kansas City has more than 300, and natives like to tout the fact they have more working fountains than Rome.

April 3rd is Fountain Day, when all the fountains are turned on for all to see. The Northland Fountain is the only fountain that flows all year.

On the day of the home opener of the Kansas City Royals baseball team, the water flows blue in all the fountains!

Walking tours with helpful, illustrated maps make this combination of water and sculpture a sight to behold.

Check out the Web site to get in the mood at www.kcfountains.org and you'll hear the water flow.

Submitted by Linda Dalton, Kansas City, Missouri

13. The Secret of the Steamboat Arabia

The discovery of 200 tons of treasure is still a secret to many, if you have not visited the Steamboat Arabia Museum in Kansas City, Missouri.

In the 1800s, steamboats traveled the Missouri River between St. Louis and Kansas City, Missouri. Between 1830 and 1895, 200 boats were lost.

On September 5, 1856, *The Arabia*, a 171-foot side-wheeler, hit a walnut tree hidden below water level that ripped through the *Arabia*'s hull. Two hundred tons of cargo that was destined for frontier merchants were destroyed. There was no loss of life except for a mule that had been tied up and went down with the ship. His skeleton was found later.

In 1987, Bob, Greg and David Hawley and Jerry Mackey found the location of the *Arabia* in a cornfield that belonged to Norman Sortor. Agreements were made, and excavation began in 1988.

The discovery was unique because the cargo remained intact. Bottled foods, liquors, perfume, fur hats, clothing, overshoes, china, glassware, buttons (shown above), thimbles and needles were just some of the many treasures. Most have been restored, but many years of restoration remain.

The joy of this discovery was the decision to share their find with the public in a well-designed museum that shows and tells their story. One visit will not be enough because their treasures will be updated. Visit their Web site to find this secret at www.1856.com.

Submitted by Jane Ponath, St. Charles, Missouri

14. The Secret of the Raphael Hotel

In 1927, in the heart of Country Club Plaza in Kansas City, Missouri, two Italian brothers who did not get along with each other decided to build a nine-story, side-by-side residential building. Its exterior architecture clearly designates its division.

In 1975, the residence was renovated and became a boutique hotel that now ranks in the top 500 hotels in the United States, according to Condé Nast's *Traveler* magazine.

Many celebrities have chosen this exclusive hotel through the years because of its privacy and quiet elegance. Adjoining the hotel in Country Club Plaza is the Raphael Restaurant, an award-winning, fine dining restaurant that features private alcoves for romantic dining.

During the Republican National Convention in 1976, the Raphael was chosen to house the Secret Service and news media. Barbara Walters and Harry Reasoner are among celebrities whom the staff fondly remember.

Visits are enjoyed by many, including one guest in 1983 who was so delighted with the hotel that she did not leave until 1991. She enjoyed a room on the first floor with a view of the Plaza, and had her own private valet and gourmet food from the house restaurant.

It is not easy to leave such company and pleasant surroundings, which include shopping and entertainment. Take a peek at www.raphaelkc.com or call for reservations at 1-800-821-5343.

Submitted by Jan Stephenson, Kansas City, Missouri

15. The Secret of the Mastodon State Historic Site

This amazing historic site is the only museum in Missouri dedicated solely to the ICE AGE. It contains an important archaeological and paleontological site: the Kimmswick Bone Bed. Bones of mastodons and other extinct animals were first found here in the 1800s. This bed gained fame as one of the most extensive Pleistocene-age deposits in the country and attracted scientific interest worldwide.

History was made in 1979 when scientists excavated a stone spear point made by hunters of the prehistoric Clovis culture in direct association with mastodon bones. This was the first solid evidence of the coexistence between the mastodon and the Clovis culture.

Faced with changing conditions, prehistoric cultures would have to develop new lifestyles and adapt to the changing environment of the late Pleistocene epoch.

Visitors can hike a trail that leads to the former excavation site. However, until the Missouri Department of Natural Resources sponsors further excavations, the remnants of the bone bed site remain safely buried

This site is located just 20 miles south of downtown St. Louis, in Imperial, Missouri. This 425-acre property provides other recreational opportunities, as well. Call 636-464-2976 for more information.

Submitted by Brooke Jackson, Imperial, Missouri

16. The Secret House on the Missouri River

A must-see visit is the Lewis & Clark Boat House and Nature Center located on the river's edge of the Missouri River, in St. Charles, Missouri. This unusual setting provides a spectacular view of the river. It also required a unique design. The lower level of the building houses the replica boats from the Lewis & Clark expedition that were centerpieces in the 2003-2006 bicentennial commemoration.

Being in the flood plain, the building has a "flow through" design to handle the periodic floods without damage to the building or obstruction of river flow. The massive size of this facility, plus the experience of seeing the life-size keelboats "up close and personal" are features you will want to share with the whole family.

The second level houses a comprehensive museum of the original Lewis & Clark expedition and bicentennial expedition that tour groups can visit. The rustic-style gift shop offers a wide variety of books and memorabilia.

The grounds surrounding the unusual building have been transformed into a nature center, showcasing native flowers, herbs, wetland plants and a forest path to explore the river setting.

This museum is open every day. Reservations for tours can be made by calling 636-947-3199. This is a secret you will want to share.

Submitted by Darold and Mimi Jackson, St. Charles, Missouri

17. The Secret Experiences in Jackson, Missouri

Missourians love a bargain as well as good food. A visit to Jackson, Missouri, invites you to a 100-mile-long garage sale that offers everything from fine antiques to flea market oddities.

Memorial Day weekend is the date when it happens. However, some get an early start on the Thursday before. You can begin the journey just south of Jackson, on Highway 25. Be cautious, as parking and pedestrians may create a safety concern.

A bigger secret in Jackson is Wib's BBQ, just two miles from Highway 25 at 1204 N. High Street. In 1948, a secret BBQ recipe was handed down to the current owners, the Hoffmans. Hickory-smoked pork shoulder is sliced very thinly and then toasted on the grill. What a great treat as you make the journey to find all those bargains.

Submitted by Lou Yeargain, St. Charles, Missouri

18. The Secrets of the St. Louis Zoo

The FREE St. Louis Zoo has been named the number 1 zoo by the Zagat Survey and *Parenting* magazine. What most people do not know are these fun facts about Missouri's St. Louis Zoo.

The zoo's free-flight, walk-through aviary, built for the 1904 World's Fair in Forest Park, inspired St. Louisans to develop the St. Louis Zoo.

More than 11,400 animals, many of them rare and endangered, live at the zoo. These 810 species represent the major continents and biomes of the world.

The St. Louis Zoo is the world leader in saving endangered species and their habitats. In 2004, the zoo launched the Wild Care Institute, which includes 12 conservation centers around the world.

The annual grocery list for the animals includes 22 tons of carrots, 13 tons of bananas, 21 tons of apples, 120 pounds of earthworms, 10 tons of mackerel, 10 tons of herring, 10,000 bales of hay, 1.3 million crickets and 1.4 tons of spinach.

Discover your own secrets by visiting the zoo at 1 Government Drive, St. Louis, Missouri, or view the Web site at www.stlzoo.org.

Submitted by Gail Zumwalt, St. Charles, Missouri

19. The Secret of the Mural City of Route 66

Cuba, Missouri, has been put on the map with its 12 beautiful murals portraying the events that happened on Rt. 66.

The beautification organization, Viva Cuba, was founded in 1984 with a goal to complete these murals by 2007 for Cuba's 150th anniversary.

The secret of the murals, however, is a story about then-15-year-old Chip Lange. Chip is an avid Civil War reenactor from Cuba who was motivated by his love for the history of the Civil War to make money for the mural, his Eagle Scout project. Seven of the murals are in a series that begins with the 1864 Battle of Pilot Knob.

Chip raised an unbelievable $36,000 for the project. He also hosted a Civil War Artillery School and Living History event, held in June 2005, that included more than 150 reenactors.

Chip and mural artist Don Gray spent many hours together on research to make sure they were historically accurate. When the "Show Me St. Louis" TV show covered the story, Don surprised Chip by painting him into the mural.

The City of Cuba has much to be proud of. The mural Web site is www.route66murals@yahoo.com.

Submitted by Norma Bretz and Catherine Lange, Cuba, Missouri

20. The Secret of Big Oak Tree State Park

Floodplains with giant trees greeted early explorers to this "bootheel" region of the state. Now the incredible "island of trees" is a sea of agriculture known as Big Oak Tree State Park.

Most folks do not realize the stature of these trees. Six trees are state champions of their species and two are registered as national champions.

There also are large, bald cypress trees in the park's cypress swamp, which is the only one of its kind in the Missouri State Park system.

As you travel the boardwalk that winds through the park's 1,029 acres, be sure to watch the birds. This park has become quite a popular spot for bird watchers.

For local information, call 573-748-5340, or travel to 13640 Hwy. 102 in East Prairie, Missouri.

Submitted by Richard Fry, Warrenton, Missouri

21. The Secret of the Mississippi River Hills

"A river runs by it." The mighty Mississippi runs by six Missouri counties that have been identified and designated by the Missouri Regional Cuisines Project, a collaborative effort based at the University of Missouri-Columbia.

The six counties are represented by the communities of Perryville, Imperial, Cape Girardeau, Kimmswick, Ste. Genevieve and DeSoto. The diversity of the river towns shows in the foods, wines, agricultural products and cultural attractions found there.

Many small towns such as Wittenberg are no longer the active river towns they once were. Towns such as Ste. Genevieve, Cape Girardeau and Kimmswick have used the river in their tourism efforts.

Maps and detailed information for touring the Mississippi include antique and craft markets, historic sites, outdoor camping and recreation, local food markets, bed and breakfast lodging, wineries, restaurants and cafés.

What a great sampling of Missouri's best! Call 1-800-292-0969 for a map or visit www.extension.missouri.edu/cuisines.

Submitted by Teresa Meier, Jackson, Missouri

22. The Best-Kept Secret in Rocheport, Missouri

Rocheport is located in mid-Missouri, just two hours east of Kansas City by car and two hours west of St. Louis. Frommer's *Budget Travel* magazine names Rocheport as one of the "coolest small towns in America."

The best-kept secret in Rocheport beside Rocheport itself is the Yates House Bed and Breakfast. It is owned and operated by Dixie and Conrad Yates and offers charming, attractive rooms in two guesthouses. One originated in the 1840s, and the other is a reproduction colonial built in the early 1990s.

What makes this establishment unique to the industry is the weekend gourmet cooking classes. Couples find them fun and romantic, as well as educational. A suggested Friday introduction to the town is a visit with the local vintner and then a quick dinner. A wine tour is planned for Saturday after breakfast, and at 2:00 p.m. prep work begins for the evening dinner. A late-afternoon break of free time is enjoyed until 6:00 p.m., when everyone returns to prepare the meal for 7:30 p.m. dinner. The B&B hosts then serve this dinner. Mary Schueter, from the Amber B&B, is Dixie's partner in this weekend adventure as well as in other catering projects.

The Yateses have outdone themselves in providing a unique, first-class experience. Check them out at www.yateshouse.com.

Submitted by John Taylor, Lee's Summit, Missouri

23. The Secret Chapel in Defiance, Missouri

The Old Peace Chapel was built in New Melle, Missouri, in the 1860s and now sits among the period buildings that comprise Boonesfield Village. It is on the grounds of Lindenwood University's Daniel Boone Home in Defiance, Missouri.

The chapel opened its doors in 1904 as Friedens Evangelical and Reform Church and then evolved into the Friedens United Church of Christ. The word *Friedens* means "peace" in German.

While the exterior is picturesque and quaint, the interior is alive with a beautiful, bright blue ceiling and pristine white walls. Wide planks of leaf red pine cover the floor, and an 1860s tower clock graces the back wall. A lovely spiral staircase leads to the choir loft above, and another spiral staircase leads to the full basement below.

A unique feature to the chapel is its new pipe organ, which contains antique parts that date as far back as the 1860s. The acoustics of the building simply must be experienced to be believed. One musician said it was like being inside a guitar.

Occasional nondenominational services are held, but the chapel is primarily used for weddings. It seats 100 people, and there is a separate building for the bride's services. More information is available by contacting one of the chapel's coordinators at 636-798-2903.

Submitted by Lynn Glancy, Defiance, Missouri

24. The Secret Record in Clinton, Missouri

What does the City of Clinton, Missouri, have that most Missourians do not know? They have the largest town square in the state of Missouri. The charm and beauty of Clinton's robust Historic District have proved that small-town squares can survive and prosper in the 21st century.

Some have described the picturesque square as a scene out of a Norman Rockwell painting.

The bandstand gazebo, originally a World War I Memorial, is situated at the northeast corner of the courthouse lawn and is still the centerpiece of local activities, just as it was 100 years ago. On the opposite corner, an original watering fountain, which refreshed horses and people alike before the coming of the automobile, is beautifully placed. Replica gaslights illuminate the square, and flower urns line the street on all four sides.

Clinton Main Street, Inc., continues to revitalize and renovate the area using the four-point approach prescribed by the National Trust for Historic Preservation. Contact the Clinton Chamber of Commerce by calling 636-885-8166.

Submitted by Sandi Cox and Diane Hannah, Clinton, Missouri

25. The Anniversary Secret of Boonville, Missouri

Many wonderful Boonville festivals are no secret to Missourians. The Big Muddy River Festival and the Missouri Arts Festival are two that draw huge crowds each year to Boonville.

The secret that connects these festivals and other events is of the Thespian Hall. It all started in 1838, when 60 Boonville men formed a dramatic club called the Thespian Society. Little did they know how their vision would develop in the next 170 years. In 1854, the benefit performances began for the building of a place of theatrical entertainment.

On July 3, 1857, this classic, Greek-revival building with massive brick columns was born. Diverse uses such as the Odd Fellows, Masons, City government, Boonville Library, Civil War Hospital, opera house and then movie theatre all adapted to its architecture.

Because the hall was always under the threat of destruction, residents were relieved when it was placed on the National Registry of Historic Places. At this time the Friends of Historic Boonville acquired the building though a gift from the Kemper Charitable Trusts. Restoration continues so that it can be a viable entity to the community. In 2007, the Thespian Hall will celebrate its 150th anniversary. Celebrate its survival and beauty!

Discover more by e-mailing friends@undata.com.

Submitted by Hallye Bone, Chesterfield, Missouri

26. The Beautiful Secret of Neosho, Missouri

On the western edge of the Missouri Ozarks in the county seat of Newton county is Neosho, Missouri. The nine springs within the city limits explain the name of Neosho: the Osage derivation meaning "clear or abundant water."

Everyone knows about its famous residents, Thomas Hart Benton, George Washington Carver and Will Rogers.

The beautiful secret unknown to most is that Neosho is known as the "Flower Box City." Flower boxes are found in abundance throughout the town, and the historic town square displays trash containers with flower boxes on top of them that are maintained by the local garden clubs. At Morse Park, north of town, you'll see a railroad car turned into a flower box.

In May, the Neosho Chamber of Commerce gives an award for the "best flower box" to encourage participation.

Each spring is the annual Dogwood Tour, when the entire countryside is adorned in redbud and dogwood trees. See for yourself at www.neoshomo.org.

Submitted by Shana Griffin, Neosho, Missouri

27. The Secret of Missouri's Farmers Market

Farmers' markets abound across the country, but Missouri has 110 markets to be proud of. They are arguably a community's best source for fresh, locally-grown produce.

One of the farmers' secrets to getting the freshest produce is picking sweet corn by the light of the moon or by car headlights before the farmers arrive early in the morning.

The old saying "the early bird gets the worm" is true not only for consumers attending the market but also for the farmers. The farmers who bring the first strawberries or the first ripe tomatoes get top dollar for their early endeavors. Dark early hours are for setting up shop as the farmers visit among their fellow farmers and neighbors.

Their personalized customer service, getting to know their repeat clientele, is one of the secrets to their continued and shared success. Communities embrace these markets with open arms as they bring the backyard gardens into our lives.

To find out where the closest farmers' market to you is located, visit http://www.grownative.org.

Submitted by Tammy Bruckerhoff, Jefferson City, Missouri

28. The Secret of Missouri's Botanical Garden

Each October, the Best of Missouri Market is held at the Missouri Botanical Garden and features more than 100 outstanding Missouri food producers, artisans and entertainers for the entire family. Visitors explore the garden and discover the best of Missouri's treasures.

The market features an array of country stands filled with fruit, vegetables, flowers, plants, herbs, nuts, candies, meats, seasonings, salsas and baked goods from Missouri's farmers and producers. Artisans offer baskets, furniture, carved birds, pottery, dried flowers, custom jewelry and soaps.

Entertainment includes a Kids Corner for activities such as carving pumpkins, milking cows and petting farm animals. Live musical performances and craft demonstrations also delight the guests.

"This market has become one of the Missouri Botanical Garden's signature events," says its Director, Dr. Peter H. Raven. "Visitors travel to be among the first to discover the best and the brightest. One of the true hallmarks of the Best of Missouri Market is that larger stores visit to identify their next new offerings."

The Missouri Botanical Garden is located at 4344 Shaw Blvd., and the phone number is 314-577-9400.

Submitted by Dr. Peter H. Raven, St. Louis, Missouri

29. The Secret Agriculture of Missouri

When someone thinks of the agricultural products of Missouri, Christmas trees don't often come to mind. For some, it comes as a surprise that farmers in Missouri plant and harvest quite a large number of Christmas trees each year.

Real trees are renewable, recyclable and resourceful, unlike artificial trees.

Missouri ranks 21st among U.S. states, harvesting 92,483 Christmas trees in 2002. This was on 3,775 acres of the 310 farms that reported to the USDA National Agriculture Census. Many more are likely to be included in an upcoming census.

Christmas tree farmers in the state grow eight different species of conifers for the market, the most common being Scotch pine, white pine, Canaan fir, white spruce and blue spruce.

There are 67 members of the Missouri Christmas Tree Association.

Providing a Christmas tradition to many is healthy and growing! "Grow Missouri" is their theme!

For more information, contact Steve Meier, President of MCTA, at meierhsp@netscape.net.

Submitted by Teresa and Steve Meier, Jackson, Missouri

30. The "Rosy" Secret of Cape Girardeau, Missouri

It may be a secret that Cape Girardeau's slogan in 1931 was "The City of Roses." For 10 miles on Hwy. 61 between Cape Girardeau and Jackson, Missouri, the highway was lined with 25,000 rose bushes. There were white roses on one side and red on the other, to represent the North and South in the Civil War.

In 1963, when work was being done on the new highway, the roses made their new home in Capaha Park. The Capaha Rose Garden, located at the corner of Perry and Parkview Streets in Cape Girardeau, has at least 38 different varieties that are maintained by local garden clubs.

National attention has been focused on this garden since it began in 1953. It was accepted as a nationally accredited rose display-testing garden in October of 1955.

Roses continue to bloom from its "rosy" past, however; Cape Girardeau's new direction is touting that Cape Girardeau is "where the river turns a thousand tales."

To experience a musical visit to the garden, visit www.rosecity.net or "Escape to Cape" by getting information at info@visitcape.com, or call toll free, 1-800-777-0068.

Submitted by Chuck Martin, Cape Girardeau, Missouri

31. The Secret of the Elephant Park

No, you are not seeing a herd of elephants. You are just seeing very large, round rocks! It is nature exposing you to some incredible, massive rocks: hot magma that over-accumulated deep below the earth's surface. Once they cooled, the red granite rocks weathered into huge, round boulders.

The number of stone "elephants" has never been counted. Some erode away, and new elephants are constantly being exposed.

"Dumbo," the patriarch of the rocks, is 27 feet tall, 35 feet long and 17 feet wide. He tips the scale at 680 tons.

A recent addition to this secret "elephant world" is a new, 450-foot trail that leads to the old engine house that was constructed in the late 1800s. This 60-foot granite structure does not have a roof, just three sides and a window enclosing the railroad line. This trail extends off the park's current Braille Trail.

There is much to do near this most unusual park. There are some 30 picnic sites that allow you to rest among the stone pachyderms. You also can see more granite buildings in nearby Graniteville, and Johnson Shut-Ins State Park is just a few miles away.

For more information call 1-800-334-6946 or visit www.mostateparks.com/elephantrock.

Submitted by Cherie Tredway, St. Charles, Missouri

32. The Secret of Charleston, Missouri

Charleston, Missouri, has a beautiful secret everyone should know about.

The Dogwood-Azalea Festival is an experience for all the senses. There are many ways to experience the incredible fragrance and color of these beautiful flowers.

During the month of April you can tour the 6-mile trail by taking a free shuttle or by arranging an entertaining and informative tour for just $35.00. A carriage ride on a pretty day also would be an entertaining and relaxing option. For a more romantic touch, you might wait until dusk, when white luminaries line the trail and azalea banks are aglow with uplights.

Many events are scheduled around this festival, such as house and garden tours, plant sales and even a quilt show. You will find many such events if you attend during the peak of the month's activities, the third weekend of April.

Also note that Charleston is the home of former Governor of Missouri Warren E. Hearnes. View items from the governor's 22 years in elected office at the Hearnes Museum.

View beautiful Charleston at www.charlestonmo.org or arrange for your tours by calling the Charleston Chamber of Commerce at 573-683-6509.

Submitted by Claudia Arlington, Charleston, Missouri

33. The Secret of Roaring River State Park

Roaring River State Park is located 7 miles south of Cassville, Missouri. At the source of the river, a spring emerges from the base of a shady limestone bluff and produces more than 20,000,000 gallons of water each day. The locals claim "the spring has no bottom."

The secret of the park of huge cliffs, steep hills and cave is a high mountaintop. Historians say it was the home of "The Mountain Maid." Some referred to her as a witch because she was an elderly lady who had "second sight." When occasional visitors would pass by, she would give them warnings, advice, or comfort by looking into their future. In 1940 she burned to death in her home. The claim "a witch will burn by fire" resonates with those who live there today.

This state park covers 3,358 acres and includes a large pool, cabins, campground, restaurant, nature center, hiking trails and more.

Call 417-847-2539 or 417-847-2330 for lodging information.

Submitted by Ann Poore, Florissant, Missouri

34. The Secret of Missouri's Most Haunted House

The Lemp Mansion, at 3322 DeMenil in St. Louis, is a haunted masterpiece that was the former home of the Lemp Brewery family. Through the years, this stately home has served in many capacities, from a boarding house to a restaurant and bed and breakfast.

What has not changed is its reputation as one of the "most haunted places in America," according to *Life* magazine. The Lemp family members are best remembered for their unusual, mysterious and untimely deaths. Visitors are reminded on a daily basis that these remaining spirits are still active and have left a ghostly legacy.

Noises, voices, transparent images, moving furniture, the sound of horses clogging and the eerie sight of candles lighting on their own are just some of the occurrences.

Charles Lemp, who committed suicide in the home, seems to be one of the most active spirits that communicates with the public, séance groups, and students of psychic phenomena.

You can visit the Lemp Mansion and enjoy delicious meals and the comforts of home. Do you dare to visit?

To learn more go to www.prarieghosts.com/lemp.html or make reservations at 314-664-8024.

Submitted by Stephen P. Walker, St. Louis, Missouri

35. The Secret of Ironton, Missouri

The secret of "hand-painted beauty" from Ironton, Missouri, is Chanticleer Pottery Studio, which is in a charming, turn-of-the-century estate next to the Misselhorn Castle. You'll find talented artists who produce beautiful and colorful roosterware or terracotta pottery.

Chanticleer means "rooster" in French, so roosters are prominently featured in the designs of dinnerware and home décor pieces, which are distributed all across the country.

Missouri is proud to present this functional art that has become such a popular collectible. See the beauty at www.chanticleerpottery.homestead.com or call the shop in Ironton at 573-546-3336.

Submitted by Debra L. Cochran, St. Charles, Missouri

36. The Secret of Hermann, Missouri

Hermann, Missouri, is known for much more than wineries. One of the best-kept secrets of that area is a retreat experience that both men and women can enjoy.

Missouri River Whitetails has one of the finest deer- and turkey-hunting vacations in the Midwest. Guided bow hunting also is a sought-after opportunity, not to mention the fishing.

Something that especially appeals to the women vacationers is the Healing Stone Retreat and Spa, perched on a bluff in a magnificent residence that offers upscale luxury services.

To accommodate both, take a look at the hunting and lodging package, the Sportsman and Lady Luxury Retreat, which blends two vacations in one. There is the trophy hunt for him and a spa sanctuary for her. A breakfast and a gourmet dinner are included, as well.

This perfect duo is just miles from the historic village of Hermann, Missouri, where you can still sample the wineries, antique shops and historic structures. Visit www.missouririverwhitetails.com or www.healingstoneretreat.com. To arrange a package, call 573-486-5000.

Submitted Anonymously

37. The Secret of Bonne Terre, Missouri

Bonne Terre Mine is the world's largest freshwater dive resort. It is designated as a National Historic Site.

The water conditions remain constant and have more than 100 feet of visibility. The lake contains 1 billion gallons of water. Rock formations are lit with 500,000 watts of lighting, which makes for a spectacular sight.

Tours are conducted for nondivers. Walking tours are conducted on the first or second levels. In the largest part of the mine, a romantic boat tour is available.

This place truly is to DIVE for!

Check it out at www.2dive.com/aboutus.com.

Submitted by Joann Cullum, Florissant, Missouri

38. The Secret of West Plains, Missouri

In West Plains, Missouri, you'll find a peaceful community called Assumption Abbey, home to a Cistercian order of monks known as the Trappists.

The Abbey is located in the rugged, wooded Ozarks. A small river flows among the hills, offering peace and seclusion.

The monks, who practice "dying" as a way of life, dress in simple clothing and eat very plain food.

A visitor can observe their normal routine, starting at 3:15 a.m. with the Office of the Vigils, 6:30 morning prayer and Eucharist, 9:00 mid-morning prayer, dinner in the commons, then dishwashing, followed by 2:00 mid-afternoon prayer, work until 4:30 p.m., 5:45 evening prayer, meditation, 7:45 p.m. Compline and then finally to bed. They do not work on Sundays, so they can enjoy reading, walks or creative activities.

The monks are known for making wonderful fruitcakes.

For travel information visit www.assumptionabbey.org.

Submitted by Kris Norman, West Plains, Missouri

39. The Secret of Dexter, Missouri

The "tea-lightful" surprise you'll find in Dexter, Missouri, is Patricia's Tearoom. Lady Patricia Shell, the owner, believes that you should take time out for family and friends. Poems and sayings are written on the walls themselves, for example: "Let us all meet each other with a smile, for a smile is the beginning of a friendship."

Patty's dream evolved from what was once a corner grocery store. Her flare for Victorian décor is quite elaborate, with tapestry chairs, floral carpeting, lace tablecloths and a variety of crystal, china and silver.

Victorian boutique items for sale are displayed everywhere throughout the room. The Sweet Treat bakery in the back of the tearoom not only has sweet delights but frozen casseroles and quiche for takeout. Upstairs you'll find Abigail's Parlor for your antiquing pleasure.

To arrange a special occasion in the tearoom or in the lovely garden in downtown Dexter, call 573-624-6887.

Submitted by Nadine Boone, St. Charles, Missouri

40. The Secret of the Wine Country Garden

Three seasons of the year, the Wine Country Garden and Nursery is a balm for the soul! From the top of a lofty hill, the view is spectacular.

The grounds are a veritable Garden of Eden that includes a working nursery and park-like setting with waterfall. A luscious, landscaped lake serves as home to the swans and ducks.

The special secret of this garden's beauty is its 3 acres of daylilies. From June to July, you can see 250 varieties in six categories and many colors that are beautiful to behold. If you choose to travel through the lily fields, guided golf-cart tours are available.

A garden gift shop is filled with goodies and 10, 000 pots of lilies are ready for purchase.

Lunch features a special chicken salad recipe that you can enjoy in the garden or on the porch of the stately home.

Themed outdoor dinners such as the Caribbean Island Feast occur throughout the summer, accompanied by ethnic music.

See the beauty at www.winecountrygarden.com or call for reservations at 636-798-2288.

Submitted by Mary Dubois, St. Charles, Missouri

41. The Secret of Missouri Golfing

The Mozingo Golf Course in Maryville, Missouri, was recognized by *Golf Digest* magazine and *USA Today* as being the "best golf course to play in the state of Missouri for under $50."

An all-day green fee for 18 holes is $20 Monday through Thursday. An all-day green fee for Friday through Sunday is only $25. This course often has been a role model for many municipal golf courses.

A unique clubhouse, driving range and practice greens are a bonus.

This course is part of the incredible Mozingo Lake Park. The 3,000 acres are included in 26 miles of shoreline surrounding a 1,006-acre lake.

If you are not up to golfing, you'll have plenty to do fishing, walking the trails or boating. A 70-site RV park and campsites help you extend your visit to one of Missouri's nature lands.

To schedule your tee time, call 660-562-3864 or visit www.mozingolf.com.

Submitted by Rick Schults of Maryville, Missouri

42. The Secret of the Jesse James Gang

The common belief about notorious bank robber Jesse James and his gang is that they were ignorant country folk with little or no moral upbringing. Although later in their careers the recruited gang members were of a tougher sort, the members of the original gang were considered to be intelligent, well spoken and religious.

The original James Gang consisted of the children of the Kansas City area's most influential people. Cole Younger was an original gang member, along with one or more of his brothers. Younger's father was a powerful Jackson County Judge.

Jesse and Frank James were the sons of Bob James, a prominent citizen of Clay County, Missouri, who helped to found the prestigious William Jewell College in Liberty, Missouri.

Additionally, according to tales told through the years, Jesse James was not only a literate man but also a well-read student of the Bible.

In later years, the gang began to attract members who were not as well heeled, such as Bob and Charlie Ford. People who knew them and their family considered them to be shiftless, worthless and ignorant, but not evil or violent.

Bob and Charlie were ultimately responsible for the death of Jesse James. Charlie shot him in the back in St. Joseph, Missouri, for a $10,000 reward and then immediately returned home to Clay County.

The Ford family stayed up all night, waiting for the James Gang to appear on their horses over the rise, ready to get their revenge, but they never showed.

Submitted by Ford descendent Jim Cates, Topeka, Kansas

43. The Secret of the Bootheel of Missouri

A very fun secret and a surprise to most of us is in Malden, Missouri. The Bootheel Youth Museum is all about having a good time and an education at the same time. This museum is for kids of all ages.

The 22,000 square-foot exhibit hall has a 180-seat theatre, children's village, space station, shadow room, classrooms, birthday room, Island Mars room and more. The newest addition is the Lewis and Clark Trail, where kids can experience all the challenges and discoveries of the trip and "meet" Thomas Jefferson, just as Lewis and Clark did.

Exploration of the arts, math and sciences, human relations and natural resources are enjoyed not only at the museum but also from an adjunct museum that travels within a 100-mile radius.

This is the ONLY museum where admission is MORE for the child than the adult. Adults are $3 and children are $5 each.

You can see the museum online at www.bootheelyouthmuseum.org or call 573-276-3600.

Submitted by Patsy Reublin, Malden, Missouri

44. The Secret of the Pony Express

The Pony Express Museum is one of the best-kept secrets of St. Joseph, Missouri. There are many interesting facts to be discovered there.

From April 3, 1860 to October of 1861, a mail relay existed between St. Joseph, Missouri, and Sacramento, California. Departures were from the east as well as the west. This route took 10 days to travel in good weather. The fastest delivery was 7 days, 17 hours between telegraph lines. This was the delivery of the Lincoln Inaugural Address.

One hundred sixty-five stations served riders who traveled 75-100 miles, when another rider would take over. This historical exercise was very difficult but captured the hearts of many before the telegraph took over.

April 3rd also is significant as the date that Jesse James was killed, exactly 22 years after the Pony Express began in 1860.

This museum is only one of 22 wonderful museums in St. Joseph, Missouri.

The Pony Express Museum is located at 914 Penn Street. Call them toll free at 1-800-530-5930 or visit at the Web site www.stjomo.com.

Submitted by Charlotte Fry, St. Charles, Missouri

45. The Secret of Joplin, Missouri

Joplin may be best known as the birthplace of George Washington Carver, but slowly word is getting around about one of its secrets.

Eleven miles southwest of Joplin is the Hornet Ghost Light, or "Spook Light," as the locals refer to it. Since 1886, this supernatural light has appeared in the middle of a long, lonely road called Spook Light Road.

The burning light has concentrated on this one road and disappears when approached, so the mystery continues.

To experience this phenomenon, take I-44 west from Joplin to Highway 43, and then drive south for approximately 6 miles until you arrive at State Road BB. You then turn right on BB and drive about 3 miles to the road's end. Turn right and then drive another mile to a second dirt road to the left. Park along that road at the darkest place you can find.

It may be a secret too scary to share!

Submitted by Adam Crumholtz, Jefferson City, Missouri

46. The Best Kept Secret of St. Charles, Missouri

The Foundry Art Centre is a fine-arts gallery overlooking the Missouri River in the Frenchtown district of historic St. Charles, Missouri. It opened in May, 2004, with a vision to become an exciting and dynamic art center.

The Art Centre features a Smithsonian-caliber gallery hosting nationally juried fine art exhibitions and curated shows.

Once a site for building and testing railcars, the Foundry has always been a place for hands-on work. Today more than 20 artists have studio galleries in the Foundry, where visitors can watch as they create paintings, pottery, jewelry, digital art and sculptures and can buy art directly from the artists.

The Children's Art Gallery exhibits art by local schoolchildren, and classes are available for them, as well.

In partnership with the City of St. Charles, the Foundry has created Art in Public Places, a program that sees to the placement of sculptures throughout the city for the public to enjoy.

This unique facility is visually exciting for special events such as weddings, private parties and corporate events. Admission is FREE, but donations are welcome. For more information, call 636-255-0270 or visit www.foundryartcentre.org.

Submitted by Joyce Rosen, St. Charles, Missouri

47. The History of Missouri Writers

If you are reading this book, you no doubt appreciate the state of Missouri and want to know more about it.

Promotion of Missouri's literary heritage can be discovered at the Missouri Center for The Book. This Missouri Center is an affiliate of the National Center of The Book in the Library of Congress, which was established in 1977. Its mission is to strengthen and celebrate the vital role of books, reading and libraries in the cultural life of the nation.

The Center's headquarters are in the Missouri State Library in Jefferson City and are governed by an independent board of directors.

There are 600 Missouri books in the center's collection. Arrangements for a Missouri Book Exhibit can be made by calling 573-751-2680.

The Web site is very helpful. You can look up your favorite Missouri author, bookstore or publisher; perhaps find out how to publish your own book.

Look, read and see at www.books.missouri.org.

Submitted by Mark W. Tiedeman, St. Louis, Missouri

48. The Secret of Chillicothe, Missouri

If you picked up the front page of the *Constitutional-Tribune* July 6, 1928, it would not be news to you that Chillicothe made the headlines in proclaiming that ...Sliced Bread Is Made Here. Chillicothe Baking Company was the first baker in the world to sell sliced bread to the public. Frank Bench's Bakery sliced the bread on a machine called the Rohwedder Bread Slicer. Bench and his partner patented their machine, but when a man in St. Louis devised a bread-wrapping method, he changed the machine just enough to be able to manufacture his own.

Chillicothe was slow to capitalize on its clever historical fact. In 2004, a committee conducted a contest, and a logo from Kim Ziegler of Chillicothe was chosen. Soon after that, the first BreadFest was planned to share the fun with the whole community.

Now you can purchase posters, "sliced bread" candles, and other memorabilia depicting this momentous discovery.

Chillicothe is a Shawnee Indian word meaning "big town where we live." Now the town is known as the "Best Thing Since Sliced Bread."

If you want to know more, call toll free at 1-888-756-0990, or look for yourself at www.chillicothecity.org/bread.html.

Submitted Anonymously

49. The Secret German Eating Spot

The town of Freistatt, Missouri, may be a secret to most of you, but Biermann's Restaurant is the secret that people are now talking and writing about. Freistatt is a German/Lutheran community of 200 that grew up around the town's 1862 hardware/country store. In 1979 it was remodeled into a restaurant. Jay Sitton, a former employee of that restaurant, came back to his hometown in 2003 to take over the restaurant and brought his German-style cooking experience with him. Jay's wife Wendy, brother Kyle and parents Linda and Jerry all help with his endeavor.

Jay's secret fried chicken batter, sweet sauerkraut, rouladin, sauerbraten, schnitzel, spaetzle (German noodles) and weiswurst are just some of the delicacies that keep this 75-seat restaurant booming. If the German menu is not for you, a hand-cut steak or his special chicken cordon bleu will delight you.

Biermann's has the kind of Missouri hospitality and cuisine that make you feel like you're in your own hometown.

You may want to visit in August when the Ernte-Fest takes place so that you can experience the whole German atmosphere.

Biermann's is located next to the Lutheran School, right in the heart of Freistatt. Take I-44 to State Rt. H at Mount Vernon, then 7 miles to Freistatt.

Visit their Web site at www.Biermannsdining.com or give them a call at 417-235-9005.

Submitted by Linda Sitton, Freistatt, Missouri

50. The Secret of Our Rivers

Our two hometown rivers, the Missouri and the Mississippi, come together at what is now the Edward and Pat Jones Confluence State Park.

Observers can see this blend of nature in the 1,118-acre park, just 2 miles downstream from where Lewis & Clark's Corp of Discovery entered the Missouri River in 1804.

The two rivers are much the same breadth, but the Missouri River is more rapid and muddy than its companion. The Mississippi River is a more vital river highway with clearer water. It is a site of nature to behold!

The confluence is one of the area's best places for bird watching because millions of birds migrate along the Mississippi flyway.

You'll be able to visit the park's interpretive center to learn about its history and beauty at 1000 River Lands Way, West Alton, Missouri. You can call for brochures and other information toll free at 1-800-334-6946.

Submitted by Donna Whitton, St. Louis, Missouri

51. The Secret Castles of Missouri

There are 18 known castles in Missouri, according to the U.S. List of Castles.

The only one open to the public is the Phythian Castle in Springfield, Missouri. A mother and daughter from out of state purchased this castle from a farmer in 1993 for $4,000. They are busy restoring this masterpiece, and they make this their residence as well as an entertainment facility and dance studio.

The 40,000-square-foot castle has a ballroom, theatre, dungeon and many bedrooms. The decorative outside walls are made of 2-foot-thick Carthage stone. Interior walls are made from a fireproof block called "Pyrobar."

The Knights of Phythian Fraternal Organization originally opened the castle as an orphanage in 1914. Many transitions occurred throughout the years. During the 1940s, Bob Hope, Stan Kenton and the Dorsey Brothers entertained troops here. During World War II, prisoners of war were kept in the dungeons. Visiting the room used as an interrogation cell many years ago will remain in your memory. Yes, in case you were wondering, the castle is certifiably haunted.

Why not check it out for yourself at 1451 East Phythian Street, Springfield, Missouri. The Web site is www.phythiancastle.com.

Submitted by Tamera Finacchiaro, Springfield, Missouri

52. The Secret of Pike County

Highway 79 in Pike County is designated as The Little Dixie Highway. It is part of the River Road, which runs along nearly all of the Mississippi River.

This National scenic drive represents the Midwest at its best, with its rolling hills, farms and small towns.

Louisiana, Missouri, is the largest town on the byway. Ten miles south is Clarksville, and north is Hannibal.

The best secret is the Dixie Highway's 50 Miles of Art. From Clarksville to Hannibal, you'll be able to visit many art galleries and artisans. This event is promoted twice a year, and as a result artists are rapidly moving to this region.

Spring and fall are the choice times to take advantage of nature's foliage and the art corridor.

For more information on the 50 Miles of Art, contact the following Chambers of Commerce: Hannibal, 573-769-0777; Louisiana, 573-754-5921; Clarksville, 573-242-3993; or visit www.50milesofart.com.

Submitted by Robert O'Shea, Louisiana, Missouri

53. The Secret of Hartsburg, Missouri

The warm community of Hartsburg, Missouri, is located on the Missouri River and the Katy Trail. Its heritage of northern European settlers has German and Dutch bloodlines. It is one of Missouri's river towns that overcame successive floods and prevailed.

If you want to count the residents, there may be just more than 2,000 people, but don't let that fool you because it attracts thousands of visitors to its Pumpkin Festival every year. This best-kept secret event goes "all out" to display thousands of pumpkins, conducts a pie-eating contest and serves delicious pumpkin delicacies and authentic homemade apple butter.

Harvest-time activities, games and a "Pumpkin King" are there for your enjoyment.

You'll be able to enjoy the river festival of the arts and visit the town's antique shops, woodcrafters, winery and restaurants.

This great fall event is the second week in October every year. Take Hwy. 63 and then State Rt. A to Hartsburg.

Peek at all the pumpkins at www.southernboonechamber.org/hartsburg.html.

Submitted by Kristen Knapp, Ashland, Missouri

54. The Secret of Park Hills, Missouri

St. Joe's State Park was once the Lead Belt of Missouri. For more than 100 years, this area produced 80% of the nation's mined lead. In 1972, St. Joe's Mineral Corporation ceased operations, and in 1976 donated the land to the state. The mining complex still stands and has been designated as the Missouri Mines Historic Site. It houses a rock and mineral museum as well as a gallery of mining equipment.

This area is a haven of 8,238 acres that are hilly and forested with persimmon trees, yucca plants, white oak, flowering dogwood and native grasslands.

The most distinctive 2,000 acres feature trails through wooded areas and sand flats, created by the sand-like residues from the lead-mining process. These trails are good for off-road vehicles, and also are appropriate for horseback riding and hiking.

It is heavily populated with wild turkey, white-tailed deer and other Missouri wildlife.

Four lakes for swimming and fishing, as well as picnic sites, are available for your enjoyment.

Directions to 2800 Pinville Road are available by calling 573-431-1069, or check the Web site www.mostateparks.com/stjoe.htm.

Submitted by Al Maiuro, St. Charles, Missouri

55. The Secret of "The Hill" in St. Louis, Missouri

In the early 1900s, Italian immigrants came from Lombardy to St. Louis and brought with them not only good food, but also a proud heritage. It shows in their stable neighborhood, called "The Hill," where their small bungalows are immaculately kept and their social ties are evident.

The secret to this close community is St. Ambrose Church (circa 1903), at 5130 Wilson Avenue. The church pays tribute to the founding immigrants with a statue placed alongside the church. This church serves as a religious, cultural, educational and social center for the community. Services are in English, but many there converse in Italian. After the church service, neighbors share their plans for the day and the latest news.

The Hill welcomes tourists and folks from all over the region who enjoy its well-known restaurants, bakeries and grocery stores.

Annual events include the religious procession of the Feast of Corpus Christi, the Columbus Day Parade, the Girodella Montanga Bike Race, and of course Hill Day.

For more about Little Italy, the Hill, visit www.shopthehill.com, or call St. Ambrose Church at 314-771-1228, for a schedule of worship services.

Submitted by Sally Faith, St. Charles, Missouri

56. The Secret of Missouri Born

The Show Me State is proud to "show and tell" about native Missourians. Missouri history will remind you of our famous political leaders, but we continue to add to our diverse and talented Missouri born.

If you are from Kansas City, you are especially proud of composer Burt Bacharach and actors Ed Asner and Jean Harlow.

Independence, Missouri, has produced a President, Harry S Truman, and also the glamour of actress Ginger Rogers.

Springfield, Missouri, is still panting over heartthrob Brad Pitt, but the previous generation was perfectly happy with actress Kathleen Turner.

St. Louis has three soap opera stars acting on "Days of Our Lives." They are in the good company of award-winning actor Kevin Kline (pictured here) and the late poet Eugene Field, as well as never-forgotten actor Vincent Price. Rapper "Nelly" certainly made the younger generation proud.

Clark, Missouri, touts General Omar Bradley. St. Joseph, Missouri, adored actress Jane Wyman and newscaster Walter Cronkite. West Plains is still bragging about country and western star Porter Wagoner. Flatt Creek, Missouri, produced actor Don Johnson, and the hit of Kennett, Missouri for always is singer Sheryl Crow.

Every day we create and debut entertainers, heroes and political leaders. How many do you know?

Submitted by Wynema Bean, St. Ann, Missouri

57. The Secret of Missouri's Traveling Fish

Did you know we have as many as 70 Missouri native fish comprising 15-20 different species that TRAVEL?

Unless the Show-Me-Missouri Fish Mobile Aquarium came to your community, you would never know that this incredible exhibit would be possible.

This mobile aquarium is 40 feet long and contains 3,200 gallons of water. The fish swim in a natural setting of rocks, logs and plants.

You could use this educational exhibit for fishing demonstrations for those who may never have had the experience of seeing a fish grab at bait. Aquatic education exposes you to sport and game fish as well as sharing the tips and techniques of fishing. The ecology of fish and their seasonal behavior can be "fishy" to say the least.

The Missouri Department of Conservation personnel are on hand to answer questions and inform onlookers of all ages.

Call the Missouri. Department of Conservation to schedule the mobile aquarium or visit www.mdc.mo.go/fish/kids/mobileaqua/ to find out where the mobile aquarium may be exhibiting.

Submitted Anonymously

58. The Secret in Fredericktown, Missouri

The Secret of Fredericktown, Missouri is St. Michael's Village. Located just north of Saline Creek, this village was established in 1799.

After the disastrous flood of 1814, most of St. Michael's was destroyed, with homes and businesses floating away from their foundations. The many people who remained went to higher ground. This community is now known as Fredericktown, Missouri, which was incorporated in 1818 and declared the seat of Madison County.

There are restored and reconstructed buildings, such as the Underriner House, built in 1837 with recycled logs on a hand-carved rock foundation. Evidence found on the first floor indicates that the north room may have been used as a trading post.

The Foundation for the Historic Preservation has been responsible for bringing this home and other early buildings from St. Michael's Village back to life.

Many communities restore their historic structures, but THIS town restored its existence. View the Underriner House at www.fhphistory.org/underrin.htm.

Submitted by Terry Sikes, Fredericktown, Missouri

59. The Secret Foundations of Missouri Wineries

Many charming Missouri wineries are located in unusual structures that were formerly other significant places.

In Weston, Missouri, the Pirtle Winery is located in a former 1867 Lutheran Evangelical Lutheran Church. Eagle Nest Winery in Louisiana, Missouri, is in a former 1880 Mercantile National Bank.

Cole Camp, Missouri, will be happy to show you Eichenbery Winery, which once was a blacksmith shop. If you visit Bland, Missouri, be sure to stop at the Wenwood Farm Winery, which is serving wine in what was a farm's dairy barn. Another "barn" winery is the Ferringo Winery in St. James, Missouri.

Many wineries are located in lovely, historic homes. The White Rose Winery, dating back to 1900 and constructed with Carthage marble, is also a Victorian bed and breakfast. LaDalee Vita Winery is in the historic 1846 Zachariah Foss House. If you want a prehistoric atmosphere, try tasting wine in a cave winery in St. Genevieve, Missouri.

There are many more wineries with original stories to tell. You can get a glimpse of all Missouri wineries at www.missouriwine.org/map.html or by calling 1-800-392-WINE.

Submitted by Jason Watkins, New York, New York

60. The Secret of Gainesville, Missouri

Gainesville, Missouri, is a town on a hill, nestled in the scenic beauty of the southern part of the Ozarks. It often is referred to as the "real Ozarks" because it remains a place for you to escape to and "get away from it all."

One of the special treats of this community is the Harlin House. The Harlin family is as historic as the city of Gainesville. The water well of the Harlin House supplied all the water for the homes on the hill in Gainesville for many years.

Built in 1912 by John Harlin, it is constructed of native walnut, oak and pine. A huge, wraparound porch is truly a signature feature of this lovely home.

The Harlin House is still in the family and has gone through various phases of restoration. The first floor of the home now serves as a charming and popular restaurant, Old Harlin House Café. Missy Harlin, John Harlin's granddaughter, has decorated the house with many family photographs and antiques. The second floor has private living space for the Harlin family's use.

Lunches are served daily, but only Friday Night Dinners are served to the happy supporters.

You can see this attractive, yellow, frame home and its restoration process on www.oldharlinhouse.com. Call for reservations at 417-679-0061.

Submitted by Barbara Greene, Gainesville, Missouri

61. The Secret of Altenburg, Missouri

In 1839, the Saxon Lutheran immigration to East Perry County, Missouri, was possibly the most organized immigration in the history of the United States.

The descendants of the original immigration still live in the rolling hills. They recently have opened 4,000 square feet of exhibit space in a new, state-of-the-art facility interpreting the history of Saxon Lutheran immigration to East Perry County and the seven original colonies, including the original log college seminary (1839), the original church building (1845) and the present Trinity Church (1867). The complex includes guided and self-guided tours, a visitor center and gift shop.

The drive to Altenburg takes tourists through the rolling hills that reminded the colonists of their beloved Saxony.

Within a few minutes of the museum is the Saxon Memorial site in Frohna, Missouri. The Wittenburg landing site and the historic Tower Rock are on the banks of the Mississippi River.

The local Tower Rock Winery and the Hemman Winery in Brazeau are close for your refreshment pleasure as you travel this historic region.

Call for directions and brochure at 573-824-6070.

Submitted by Larry Degenhardt, St. Louis, Missouri

62. The Secret of the St. Louis Arch

The nationally known symbol of Westward Expansion is the St. Louis Arch. It is the tallest monument in the National Park System, measuring 630 feet in height. Millions of visitors make this a must-see experience when they visit St. Louis, Missouri.

The secret surprise to visitors is The Museum of Westward Expansion. The Arch's foundation sinks to 60 feet underground. The museum is located below the Arch and has been compared to the size of a football field.

The museum contains an overview of the Lewis and Clark Expedition, a collection of artifacts, mounted animal specimens and an authentic Native American teepee.

The museum is most proud of its accreditation, which is the highest honor bestowed by the American Association of Museums of Washington, D.C. Of 8,000 museums nationwide, only 750 are accredited.

Many hours can be spent viewing the exhibits, watching videos or shopping in the wonderful gift shop. There is plenty to do for the "fear of heights" visitor while waiting for others to go up to the top of the Arch.

Submitted Anonymously

63. The Secret of Independence, Missouri

The unusual secret in this historic community, known as President Harry Truman's hometown, is a museum that is the only one of its kind in the nation. Leila's Hair Museum is devoted to an art form that died out in the early 1900s.

This newly expanded and rare museum will amaze you with more than 300 hair wreaths, men's and women's jewelry, historic photos, the history of hair and hair samples from well-known celebrities.

Leila, the owner, says that the oldest piece she owns is a hair brooch that dates back to 1680.

Her knowledge and her extensive collection have inspired her to write three books. They are a children's book, a how-to book on making hair wreaths and her latest book on hair genealogy. She claims that before the invention and widespread use of the camera, prior to 1838, saving hair was a way of keeping family history.

This "hair-raising" experience will no doubt be one of the more unusual secrets for you to discover in Missouri.

The museum is closed on Sundays and Monday, but open from 9:00 a.m. to 4:00 p.m. Tuesdays through Saturdays. It is located at 1333 S. Noland. If you'd like to call, the phone number is 816-833-2955.

Submitted by Diane Brockman, Independence, Missouri

64. The Secret of Eminence, Missouri

One of the most frequently visited Ozark springs, because of its picturesque setting, is Alley Spring. Once known as the Barksdale Spring, its name changed when a new owner purchased the land in 1870. It holds the record for the largest credible measured flow of any Ozark spring.

The spring has a famous gristmill, built in 1868, that has had many owners over the years. The mill evolved somewhat with technology until its closing in 1918. Originally it was unpainted, and then painted white with green trim. Now, in striking barn red, it has become one of Missouri's most photographed historic sites.

The 407 acres, which included the spring and mill, were sold to the new park system and are now part of the Ozark National Scenic Riverways. The gristmill equipment is on display, and the National Park Service operates a store in the mill that sells related merchandise.

Eminence has been named one of the 50 Best Outdoor Sports Towns in the United States by *Sports Afield* magazine, and proudly claims Alley Spring and the Alley Roller Mill among its most special attractions.

The Mill is open daily from Memorial Day through Labor Day. It's located just 6 miles west of Eminence on Highway 106. Call for more information at 573-226-3318.

Submitted by Susan Orchard, Eminence, Missouri

65. The Secret of the St. Louis Cathedral

One of the most under-publicized attractions in the St. Louis area is the Cathedral Basilica of St. Louis. Archbishop John Glennon began the building of this expression of faith in 1907. Catholic worship in this unique architecture of Romanesque style on the exterior and Byzantine style in the interior certainly got the attention of its followers.

The amazing secret that any tourist from around the world would want to behold is its mosaic art. It starts at the narthex, but the real beauty is yet to be discovered in the main body of the church. The great center dome above and the lesser domes and half domes, together with the arches, reveal in mosaic the story of the Catholic faith from Creation to the Last Judgment.

This is the largest collection of mosaic art in the world, created by 20 different artists and totaling 83,000 square feet. The installation contains 41.5 million pieces of glass tesserae using more than 700 colors. The installation process began in 1912 and was not fully completed until 1988.

Additional information on the creation of the mosaics and construction of the Cathedral are displayed in the Mosaic Museum on the lower level. The burial crypt of John Cardinal Glennon also is located in the museum.

The Cathedral Shop is in the west vestibule, where visitors try to capture what they have just seen and hope to bring home. The Cathedral is a visual beyond your belief.

The tours are free, Monday-Friday; weekend tours must be arranged in advance by calling 314-373-8241. The museum and shop hours are from 10:00 a.m. – 4:00 p.m.

Submitted by Doris McCall, Florissant, Missouri

66. The Secret of Versailles, Missouri

The First Saturday in October is the Old Tyme Apple Festival in Versailles, Missouri. More than 30,000 visitors flock to this small, charming town of just 2,500 people. The apple is celebrated in many creative ways.

Most do not know that *Rural Missouri*, a statewide publication of the Association of Missouri Electric Cooperatives, voted the Apple Festival the Best Festival in the state of Missouri for many years.

The festival is chock full of a variety of foods, fun and entertainment. The apple pie contest will make your mouth water; the pie-eating contest may have another effect.

Versailles also is known for its Mennonite community. The Mennonites participate in the festival by selling and displaying their quilts, woodwork and baked goods. There are 400 booths lining the town square.

You may meet the Apple Festival King or Queen or the Baby Dumpling contest winner. Many other events lead up to this all-American celebration of the apple.

For more information, call the Versailles Chamber of Commerce, 573-378-4401.

Submitted by Sherrie Johnson, Versailles, Missouri

67. The Secret of New Town at St. Charles

The white obelisk welcomes you into New Town and the circle drive makes you slow down and take in the view of an "old town." As you follow the canal, lined with black, cast-iron bollards, the first thing you notice is the mixture of housing types—lakefront homes, apartments, cottages, row homes, custom homes, town homes, work/live units and single-family homes. The architecture and the colors are quite eye-opening. The lakes and the fountains provide a water element that is welcoming and soothing. The bridges provide a European feel.

As you continue your drive, you notice that the streets are narrow and more suited to pedestrians than cars. That's when you notice people on their front porch swings talking to their neighbors. Couples are walking their dogs and some parents are tossing a baseball back and forth with their children at the outdoor amphitheatre. Residents gather at the mail center to pick up their mail. Families are riding bikes. Joggers wave and smile to folks having lunch at the bookstore's café court. Shoppers are coming out of the general store, carrying tote bags full of groceries and walking home.

The secret of New Town is people. …PEOPLE OUTSIDE. People interacting with other people in a community designed just for that purpose.

Submitted by Richard Kennison, St. Charles, Missouri

68. The Secret in the Mark Twain National Forest

A secret so hidden and yet so international is the living artist from the Brushy Creek Pottery and Botanicals. Ken George, a world-traveled artist who settled in the Missouri Ozarks more than 20 years ago, is hidden in a world of nature that produces functional and decorative pottery. He formulates his own glazes and has many kinds of kilns. He prefers to use wood-fire kilns, as they did many years ago. Mother Nature and his forest environment are his inspiration.

His most treasured creation is the Serenity Series, which has hand-painted scenes of the Ozarks created with masterful attention. The first piece in the series is on display in the Missouri Sate Capitol in Jefferson City, where it represents Missouri Fine Arts.

Ken's work is available for purchase only online at www.brushycreekpottery.com.

Ken's many talents are now available through the "Pottery the Art" program on the Web site, on which he offers pottery instructions as well as one-on-one assistance. Many schools and universities find this site a useful tool for teaching the art of pottery.

Ken would prefer that you visit him on the Web, at his availability, rather than visit him in his secret community of Ellsinore, Missouri, a town of only 363 people. You also may call him at 573-322-8205.

Submitted by Ken George, Ellsinore, Missouri

69. *The Secret of Bolivar, Missouri*

One of the most beautiful and amazing places to visit in Bolivar, Missouri, is the Dunnegan Gallery of Art at 511 N. Pike Street.

Visitors come from the five state areas to visit this contemporary structure that houses exclusive and permanent collections.

The gallery hosts Arts for the Parks as well as the National Park Academy of the Arts, which is a national tour of the top 100 paintings selected every year. This tour travels to eight locations across the United States.

The permanent collection of Southwest art, along with the impressive bronzes, woodcarvings and sculptures, makes this a cultural must see.

Bolivar is 35 miles north of Springfield, Missouri. For more information about currents exhibits, call 417-326-3438, or e-mail the Bolivar Chamber of Commerce at bolchamb@altel.net.

Submitted by Diana Leslie, Bolivar, Missouri

70. The Secret Trail of Pickle Springs

A most memorable trail through time is Pickle Springs. This natural area has one of the most spectacular scenic trails in Missouri. The National Park Service named this spring a Natural Landmark in 1974. Local legend has it that the area is named after William Pickles, a settler from Illinois who was killed by renegades during the Civil War.

The popularity of this trail is due to its forested gorge, which has geological formations and plants found in few other places. Among the natural bridges, you'll find blooming azalea and other wildflowers that are most impressive.

In this do-able 2-mile hiking trail, you'll find strategically placed benches that are the result of a recent Eagle Scout project.

Pickle Springs and other creeks flow into Pickle Creek, which flows into Hawn State Park.

From I-55 you pass Hawn State Park and continue to County Road AA. Follow for 1 mile to Dorlac Road, and then about a half-mile to the parking lot. Call 573-290-5730 for more information.

Submitted by Joani Narayan, Manchester, Missouri

71. The Secret Sunken Montana Riverboat

The *Montana* riverboat was built in Pennsylvania in 1878 or 1879 and sank in the Missouri River in 1884. Curiosity seekers, riverboat enthusiasts, news media and archeologists continue to keep her legend alive. The *Montana* is the only sunken riverboat in the St. Louis area that gets this amount of attention.

Her popularity is due to her large size, the location of her sinking, and the fact that her skeleton always reemerges when the water level drops. She was the first large riverboat to navigate the Missouri River to Ft. Benton, Montana, delivering a record load of 600 tons of cargo. She remains a secret except to the very determined individuals who seek her out. Many look for her but do not find her. There are no signs identifying her location and there are no roads. The *Montana* can be seen only on an unpredictable schedule when the river level is low; otherwise only muddy water is seen.

The mystique surrounding the *Montana's* sinking is that she was in a losing battle with the railroads. She was created too late to be competitive. Did she "commit suicide" by "falling into the railroad's sword" that was in her territorial waters? She crashed into a railroad bridge pier, thereby admitting defeat. Or did she hope to collapse the railroad bridge by breaking a support pier? We can speculate, but only the *Montana's* ghost knows for sure.

You can read more about the *Montana* in the book *The Legendary Montana Riverboat*. E-mail noweber@juno.com or call 636-677-8972 for more information.

Submitted by Nelson O. Weber, St. Charles, Missouri

72. The Secret of Missouri's Covered Bridges

There are four historic covered bridges in the state of Missouri, and all have secrets to be told.

The Locust Creek Covered Bridge was built in 1868. It had a long history of flooding and channel meandering, so over the years it was raised three times, by approximately 15 feet in all. Farmers of Laclede, Missouri, needed to be able to get their goods to the railroad stations, so the longest bridge of the historic four is 151 feet long.

The Buford Covered Bridge is part of the Bollinger Mill State Historic site and is the oldest remaining covered bridge, constructed in 1858. It is a pedestrian-only bridge that spans the Whitewater River, and is 140 feet long and 12 feet wide. It is located in Cape Girardeau County, Missouri.

The Union Covered Bridge was built in 1871 in Stoutsville and is located at the Mark Twain Birthplace State Historic site.

The Sandy Creek Covered Bridge is the newest of the existing bridges. This 1872 barn red favorite can be seen in Imperial, Missouri.

I think you need to UNCOVER them all! The locator map is www.mostateparks.com/statemap.htm.

Submitted by Denzil Heaney, Laclede, Missouri

73. The Secret of the Luxenhaus House Farm

Little did Lois and Bill Hostkoetter know in 1973 that the 1820s frontier log cabin that they purchased as a home in Perryville, Missouri, would someday be the beginning of a village for German culture.

There are at least 30 log cabins now on the farm. All were donated and constructed by volunteers. National magazines such as *Country Home* and *Country Living* have published features on this marvelous German village.

It is now the home of Deutsch Country Days, which take place on the third weekend in October. The hills come alive with the sights and sounds of the 1800s. Authentically costumed craftsmen demonstrate domestic tasks such as rug braiding, candle dipping, natural dyeing and woodworking. Period music and the fragrance of sorghum cooking set the scene of the Missouri mules and steam-powered sawmill, portraying the German heritage.

The future of this amazing place is the creation of the Folk Art School. Thirteen artisans teach the period topics in the middle of August. To register or find more information on this school and its festivities, call 636-433-5669 or e-mail info@deutschcountrydays.org

Submitted by Lois Hostkoetter, Marthasville, Missouri

74. The Secret of the Museum Without Walls

Laumeier Sculpture Park is not only a museum without walls, because it is outdoors, but it is also home to the largest outdoor display structures available all year 'round in Missouri.

Originally a 72-acre gift from Matilda Laumeier in 1968, the park was expanded to 98 acres in 1975 by a group of civic leaders. It also includes a large, historic, stone-cut home.

Laumeier Sculpture Park, accredited by the American Association of Museums, is an institution of international significance. Many artists of international acclaim have work displayed there.

It is one of few institutions that primarily collects monumental and site-specific contemporary sculpture as its main focus.

"The Way" by artist Alexander Liberman is an example of the park's dramatic structures. It is 65 feet tall and 100 feet wide. Made of steel, its column components are painted red.

The "Creation Location" site is the location of one of the park's popular annual events, the Laumeier Sculpture Park Art Fair, held every May. It provides art demonstrations and hands-on art-making activities for more than 5,000 children each year. All varieties of food and art are enjoyed, with wine tasting from Missouri wineries.

Admission is free, except for special events. The park is located at 12580 Rott Road in St. Louis County. You may call 314-821-1209 or visit at www.laumeier.org.

Submitted by Jennifer Duncan, St. Louis, Missouri

75. The Secret of Florissant, Missouri

The Taille de Noyer home is the oldest home in St. Louis County, dating back to 1790. "Taille de Noyer," meaning a "clearing in the walnut grove," was part of a Spanish land grant.

In 1808, John Mullanphy, known as St. Louis' first millionaire, purchased the property. The property later went to his daughter, Jane Chambers, in 1819; she and her husband added onto the home for their 17 children. The family's descendants lived in the house until 1961, when the land was donated to the Ferguson-Florissant School District. They had to move the home 200 yards to make room for the McCluer High School campus.

The home contained many authentic, unique pieces, such as a St. Louis Merkel and Mersman piano.

Visitors many times say that they feel they are visiting a home rather than a museum run by the Florissant Historical Society. It also hosts an annual Christmas luncheon and is featured yearly at the popular Florissant Valley of the Flowers Festival.

For tours and more information, at 314-524-1100.

Submitted by Debbie Wolfersberger, Florissant, Missouri

76. The Secret of Carthage, Missouri

Historic Route 66 represented Missouri in all it had to offer for business and entertainment, including drive-in theaters. At one time there were as many as 35 drive-ins on Route 66.

The last surviving drive-in on Route 66 is in Carthage, Missouri, at 1723 Old 66 Boulevard. The Goodmans have owned the drive-in since 1985, but held a grand reopening in 1997 with vintage cars and ceremonial "film cutting" by Route 66 author and historian Rob Roy. Vendors also peddled Route 66 memorabilia.

There are approximately eight drive-ins still in operation in the state of Missouri. This nostalgic form of entertainment has recently recaptured a younger audience who may never have experienced the "car movie" and concession stands of great snacks were it not for the efforts of people like the Goodmans. It is wholesome entertainment for the whole family and a great bargain that most people can afford.

To find out what movie is playing, you can call 417-359-5959 or visit their Web site at www.comevisit.com/66drivin

Submitted by Mark Goodman, Carthage, Missouri

77. The Secret of the Honey Branch Garden

This lovely Ozark property includes two caves, the Big Honey Branch Cave and Honey Branch Cave.

The larger cave is the "show cave." It has a beautiful natural waterfall and seven man-made waterfalls.

The original purpose of the Honey Branch Garden was to create an educational hosta garden. One hundred different species of hosta plants are on display, as well as unusual grasses and thousands of annuals.

These caves are no longer open to the public, but what developed out of this natural beauty was The Garden of Dreams. This cave creates a lovely setting for weddings that includes an altar of flowers, candles and all the trimmings for a beautiful wedding. Bookings are taken from the end of April to the end of October. The owners, Jody and Bill Roston, purchased the property in 1993 and claim that the weather is always perfect for weddings.

For wedding arrangements you can call 417-683-3733 or e-mail the Rostons at roston@tri-lakes.net. Their hidden secret is a "beauty."

Submitted by Jan Lewien, St. Charles, Missouri

78. The Secret of Cole Camp, Missouri

Cole Camp, Missouri, is where the Ozarks meet the great prairies of Benton County. The downtown area, listed on the National Registry of Historic Places, and the site of one of the first Battles of the Civil War, is where you'll find the Buzzards Roost Woodcarving Shop. Jim and Marge Maxwell own this "old time" shop. Jim is a 30-year master craftsman and woodcarver and Marge is a talented painter.

In the surroundings of a downtown country store, you'll enjoy watching the Maxwells carve and paint woodcarvings from 2 inches to as tall as 3 feet or more. The attractive carved Indian outside the shop entrance is an example of their fine work.

Jim is the author of four woodcarving books with original patterns and tips from Marge on wood painting. Seminars also are offered, as well as wood carving supplies and services. Started blanks are available for sale, with instructions for finishing.

The Buzzard's Roost Woodcarving Shop is in a historic structure at 113 West Main Street. Call 660-668-2466.

Submitted by Marie Viebrock, Cole Camp, Missouri

79. The Secret of Uniontown, Missouri

You receive more than the pleasure of antiquing in an 1800s store when you visit the Country Charm Emporium in Uniontown, Missouri. The Thompsons, owners since 1997, will educate you with the incredible history of the Frentzel Country Store.

Charles and Amelia Frenzel, who emigrated from Germany in 1839, opened the store in 1855.

A record of the first day's business is displayed in a ledger in which it is written that they sold a clock for $4.50, two yards of cloth and six buttons.

Ownership passed to a nephew, Paul Hopfer, and then the store was sold to Hugo and Melva Winters. It was known as the "Winters Store" for some time.

The new owners have revived the retail component to the building, but it still is heated with a wood-burning stove and has no plumbing.

Visitors are few, as they pass through this little town, known as Paitzdorf until the Civil War, then renamed Uniontown. A trail of other interesting small communities will enhance your visit to this River Heritage Region. The Country Charm Emporium is located on Highway 61, next to the Uniontown Post Office. It is open only on weekends. Call 573-788-2291 for more information.

Submitted by Diana Thompson, Cape Girardeau, Missouri

80. The Secret of Missouri's Tree Houses

If you never played in a tree house growing up, it's not too late! You can now stay in a "grownup" tree house at the River of Life Farm in Dora, Missouri.

The McKee family lives on and operates a business at this paradise farm, located in the heart of the Wild Trout Management Area of the North Fork of the White River Missouri Ozarks. One mile of bank access to prime wild rainbow trout fishing is exclusive to the farm's guests.

After the success of building their first tree-house cabin, the Hideaway Treehouse, the Mountain Lookout Cabin, the Treetop Cabin, the Eagle's Nest Cabin, the Cedar Chest Cabin and the Chalet Lodge followed. Each has a style unique to the tree itself. A conference center also is available for groups or meetings.

All of these cabins overlook the beauty of nature at its best. It's where private, peaceful and romantic experiences take place, unless a thunderstorm kicks up, and then it's a view you will never forget.

The River of Life Farm (ROLF) can take you to new heights that only the birds experience. Discover more offerings on their Web site, www.riveroflifefarm.com, or call 417-261-7777.

Submitted by Ann McKee, Dora, Missouri

81. The Secret of Missouri's Arrowheads

Where are Missouri's elusive arrowheads? Most people do not realize the large population of Native Americans that inhabited our state and how they lived, hunted and fought over campsites and hunting grounds for hundreds of years.

People who hunt these relics are very tight lipped about their favorite hunting sites, fearing that others will move into their territory and that landowners will make them leave.

The prime hunting sites are along the rivers and streams in our state. These waters provided food, drinking water and transportation. High grounds and fields along the tops of bluffs overlooking the water are good places to hunt for arrowheads, but not in the fields that flood on a regular basis. A freshly plowed field is the best place to look, especially after a good rain.

Flint chips and flakes are the best sign of an Indian campground. It is hard to find a good worked flint, but broken ones are abundant.

Most importantly, permission must be granted from the landowner to search his or her land. Be mindful of any planted crop and watch your step as you enjoy the thrill of the past.

For more information on Missouri's arrowheads, call 636-677-2336.

Submitted by Ed Horton, Fenton, Missouri

82. The Secret of "Missouri Day"

Did you know we have a designated day in Missouri when we celebrate our state? This is a secret all Missourians should know about.

In 1913, Anna Brosius Korn, a native Missourian and civic activist, visited Jefferson City with her drafted resolution for the inauguration of Missouri Day. She thought it should be celebrated in the fall because Mark Twain said, "Missouri is at her best in October." Anna knew that the goldenrod, the state flower at that time, was blooming and that harvesting was over. The bill passed and was approved by Governor Elliot Mayor on March 23, 1915.

On June 27, 1969, an amendment to section 9.040 was made to move Missouri Day to be the third Wednesday of each October.

The day is for Missouri people in educational, commercial, political, civic, religious and fraternal organizations to devote part of the day to the methodical consideration of the products of the mines, fields, and forests of the state. It also is dedicated to the consideration of the achievements of the sons and daughters of Missouri in commerce, literature, statesmanship, science and art, and in other departments of activity in which the state rendered services to mankind.

Mark it on your calendar, for Missouri is a good place to visit, live and work.

Submitted by Department of the Secretary of State, Jefferson City, Missouri

---

THE SONG OF MISSOURI

All praise to old Missouri,
To her people staunch and true;
To the flag that floats above her,
Of the red, white and blue.
And honor to our country,
And our God whom we adore;
Whose guidance we petition,
Henceforth forevermore.

83. The Secret of Our Missouri Baskets

The much sought-after Missouri white oak basket is known world-wide for its durability and good looks. It begins with white oak trees that grow on the north-facing slope of Missouri hillsides. Using techniques applied for generations, basket makers split logs into a billet with froe and mallet. A drawknife is used to shape the rough-split billet into a board, which then is sliced into very thin strips of oak that will be woven into a native white oak basket.

White oak is just one of many materials that can be woven into a basket. The spectrum of natural and synthetic materials is wide and lends itself to a huge diversity of shapes, sizes and type. Current Missourians keep the ancient craft of basket weaving alive through the Missouri Basket Weavers Guild, dedicated to perpetuating the art of basketry and stimulating interest in the historic craft. Each member shares a common spoke or thread in his or her passion for basketry.

The development of what is now known as the Missouri Basket Weavers Guild, Inc., began in 1990. Current membership is 350. More information about the Missouri Basket Weavers Guild and its weaving conventions can be found at www.mbg.unionpoint.net.

Submitted by Marilyn Margrave, Raymore, Missouri

84. The Secret of Missouri's Beers

In the 1800s, German immigrants brought their brewing skills to America. One of the largest industries in Missouri is brewing beer. In 1810, Jacques St. Vrain opened the first brewery north of St. Louis. Missouri had many caves for keeping beer cool, and plenty of water. Other breweries in municipalities around the state soon followed. Many of them closed during Prohibition and reopened at a later time.

Today we are more "up close and personal" with microbreweries, where different tastes can be explored, unlike national brands. Micro beer often is promoted for its freshness.

These microbreweries usually are located in historic buildings of substantial size, like the Trailhead Brewing Company in St. Charles, which is housed in an 1800s tobacco and feed mill. The Flat Branch Pub and Brewery is in a 1927 brick warehouse in Columbia and was voted #1 microbrewery by *Rural Missouri* magazine. Dozens of ales, beers and ciders are brewed right on site, and great lunch and dinner menus are offered, as well.

More than brewpubs and microbreweries are here in Missouri to carry on the tradition. Go to www.beer100.com/brewpubguide.htm to find out more.

Submitted by Joel H. Watkins IV, St. Charles, Missouri

85. The Secret of the Hidden Shrine

Nestled in the hills of the Heritage River Region is Apple Creek, Missouri. German Catholic immigrants settled here in the 1820s and established St. Joseph Parish. As it changed architecturally over time, so did the secret shrine behind the church.

Father Mitchell Deck began the development of the shrine in the 1950s. Parishioners did most of the stonework, using foundations from old farm homes and barns in the community.

The shrine boasts a magnificent 20-foot waterfall that disappears into an underground river and cave. An altar with a statue of Mary, Our Lady of Grace, is placed on a cliff above the waterfall.

An impressive walkway with carved wooden Stations of the Cross will lead you to this beautiful setting, perfect for meditations, prayer or ceremonies.

Mysterious occurrences have been reported in this sacred spot, like the story of the yellow butterfly, and the smelling of the roses.

You must see this inspirational spot that very few have discovered, other than local parishioners.

Just take the Biehle exit from Hwy. 55, and then take Hwy. B west 1 mile to State Road F. Then go east 5 miles to Apple Creek. Call for tour information at 573-788-2258.

Submitted by Mary Jane Buchheit, Old Appleton, Missouri

86. The Secret of Missouri's Cowboys

Missouri is the Gateway to the West, and wagon trains left from stations at Independence, Westport, St. Joseph and other western Missouri cities.

The traditional culture of the cowboys of Missouri came to life when the Missouri Cowboy Poet Association was founded in 1996. Four men from Louisburg, Mexico, Verona and Savannah, Missouri, agreed that it was time to unite and preserve the history of the cowboy and promote cowboy poetry.

The organization presented the Missouri State Library in Jefferson City with 176 copies of their publication to be delivered to every state-operated library in Missouri. They all arrived in cowboy fashion in a covered wagon to deliver their book, *Missouri Cowboy Poetry*. Proceeds from the book sales benefit an annual $1,000 scholarship. The secret of the "lonesome cowboy" is out! For information call 417-498- 6865 or e-mail the association at lwatts@mo-net.com.

Submitted by LeRoy Watts, Verona, Missouri

87. The Secret of Breckenridge, Missouri

Sitting prettily on a lakeside, 1,200-acre ranch is the Rafter P. Ranch Historic Home formerly owned by J.C. Penney, founder of the famous national chain of department stores.

Carolyn and Wes Peterson now own this stately home in Northwestern Missouri. Carolyn and her sister, Christy Savage, have opened the estate as a Bed and Breakfast and quilting retreat facility. This presents an opportunity for the sisters to offer their professional skills as teachers and antique appraisers to students from far and wide.

Weekend retreats are arranged for your stay in great rooms furnished with antiques and linens. Full breakfasts, luncheons, afternoon teas and a wonderful dinner are some of the perks to the retreats. Quilt workshops are held in the spacious garden cottage, adjacent to this famous historic home. A walk around the lake adds to the serenity of this getaway.

The whole experience is promoted as "Quilting in the Country" in one of Missouri's famous landmarks.

To visit on the Web, go to www.hameltonmissouri.us/quilt/quilt.htm, or call Carolyn at 660-644-5510.

Submitted by Thersa Heim, Breckenridge, Missouri

88. The Secret of Famous Missourians

Many Missouri communities have their own celebrities, heroes or other hometowners they consider "famous" by local standards, but there are also many Missourians who have made outstanding contributions to the world.

In 1982, the Missouri Capitol Society, Inc., created the Hall of Famous Missourians, overseen by the Speaker of the House, currently Rod Jetton.

Representing our greatest are 25 beautiful bust sculptures displayed on the third-floor rotunda of the Capitol building in Jefferson City.

Among those represented are Davis Rice Atchison, Josephine Baker, Thomas Hart Benton, Susan Elizabeth Blow, General Omar N. Bradley, Samuel Langhorne Clemons, Walter Elias Disney, George Washington Carver, James Cash Penney, Scott Joplin, Joyce C. Hall, Emmett Kelly, Reinhold Niebuhr, Charlie "Bird" Parker, General John J. Pershing, Sacajawea, Harry S Truman, Laura Ingalls Wilder, Ewing Marion Kaufmann, Walter Cronkite, Tom Bass, James "Champ" Clark, Stanley Frank Musial, Edwin Hubble and, most recently, Jack Buck.

Sculptors William J. Williams and Sabra Tull Meyer have created remarkable likenesses of these Missourians.

To find out more, go to www.house.mo.gov/famous/default.axpx or visit the Capitol in Jefferson City, Missouri.

Submitted Anonymously

89. The Secret of the Corn Cob Pipe Museum

The Missouri Meerschaum Company is the largest manufacturer of corncob pipes in the world and began the tradition for which the river town of Washington, Missouri, became famous.

The history and memorabilia of the corncob pipe are to be found in the Corn Cob Pipe Museum, a large room with a back-door entrance in Washington. The mosaic wall that incorporates hundreds of pipes and cigar holders is mounted on what is now worn velvet. This was created by employees of the factory weeks before it was entered for competition in the Research and Industry category for the St. Louis World's Fair in 1904.

This intricate design won a gold medal that was awarded to the original owner of the factory, the H. Tibbe & Son Company. The ornate, framed certificate is signed by the president of the Louisiana Purchase Exposition, David R. Francis.

The creativity and handiwork of the factory workers has been continuous since 1869. White hybrid corn, raised on 140 acres owned by the company, helps to create a larger cob. Approximately 5,000 handmade pipes are shipped daily to every state and some countries.

You can visit this museum weekdays, 8:00 a.m. to 3:00 p.m., at 400 Front Street in historic downtown Washington, Missouri. Call 636-239-2109 for more information. Tours of the factory are not offered.

Submitted by Kathy Maune, Washington, Missouri

90. The Secret of Missouri's Frogs

Helen Claypool of Kirksville, Missouri, finds that it is easy "being green" when it comes to her collection of frogs in many shapes and colors.

If frogs are sparse in your part of the state, they probably are congregating in Helen's House of Frogs museum and gift shop. Visitors can expect to see the biggest collection of frogs in the country. More than 14,000 frogs are catalogued and photographed in her 47 albums. Included are more than 300 brooches, 25 watches, 50 rings, pepper shakers, thimbles, purses, cookie jars and yard ornaments.

Her largest frog is 4 feet high, made out of a wooden log, and welcomes her visitors. Her smallest frog is in a ring set.

Helen has created more than 200 frog molds for which she sells patterns in her gift shop, which is paired with the museum. When not attending frog collectors' conventions, she and her husband, referred to as "Mr. Toad," are scouting for more frogs on the road or the Internet.

There is no charge to visit 21745 Potter Road in Kirksville, but do call ahead at 660-627-3764 or e-mail Helen at frogh@cablenet.net.

Submitted by Donald Claypool, Kirksville, Missouri

91. The Secret of the 1940's Village

In 1944, when the U.S. military decided to construct housing for its local officers, 36 charming, colonial, white, two-story houses were built in what we call today a "gated community." It had a private road to the processing plant where the officers worked.

The attractive, tree-lined village, known as Weldon Springs Heights, was purchased by a private investor in 1950 but continued to offer the homes to military families. Steve Heitkamp, born in the neighborhood, is the third generation to live there.

The community has embraced the challenges of improvements and additions, as it has become a close-knit neighborhood.

The highlight of the year is the 4th of July celebration, which includes a prayer service in one neighbor's yard; then visiting begins in other yards with a variety of entertainment. Turtle races, egg-tossing contests and cakewalks are just a few of the activities, but the tug of war is everyone's favorite. All the neighbors participate in the parade. If it moves and it's decorated, it is eligible for a prize.

No, it's not a movie like "The Truman Show." It's "Weldon Springs Heights" in Weldon Springs, Missouri, located off Hwy. 40, west of the Missouri River. Call 636-300-1637 for more information.

Submitted by Steve Heitkamp, Weldon Springs, Missouri

92. The Secret of Vintage Hill Farm

Six miles off the beaten path of Boonville, northwest on Hwy. 87, are a secret garden and farm that await you. This 100-acre paradise offers unique experiences and a huge amount of garden varieties to choose from.

Vintage Hill Farm boasts 1,700 kinds of plants, 30 different tomato plants, more than 1,000 kinds of annuals, 60 cultivars of coleus, 90 varieties of roses, and many unusual tropical plants. These all are grown locally on the farm. Shrubs, trees and evergreens are offered, but these are brought in seasonally.

Owners Jeff and Ann Oberhaus live on the farm in a restored 1900s farmhouse. The grounds include six greenhouses, an extensive equine business and rugged hillsides, where you'll find Highland cattle grazing with mares and foals.

You'll also want to visit the extensive gift shop, which features unusual pottery and garden gifts.

Seasonal hours of operation are 9:00 a.m. to 5:00 p.m. daily. The farm is open in the spring from March 1- June 30 and in fall from September 1-October 31. Browse the Web site, www.vintagehill.com, or e-mail to info@vintagehill.com.

Vintage Hill Farm is located between Boonville and Glasgow, Missouri.

Submitted by Jeff Oberhaus, Franklin, Missouri

93. The Secret of Missouri's Mushrooms

Ask the people of Richmond, Missouri, why it is called the Mushroom Capitol of the World. They proclaimed the title in 1980 because nowhere else can you pick bushels of morel mushrooms in the spring as you can in Richmond. A few cities in the United States try to proclaim the title, but Richmond is the place that is flooded with the mushroom hunters each year.

Richmond annually celebrates with a Mushroom Festival. The festival's 26th anniversary was marked in 2006. Typical festival activities are highlighted with the theme of the mushroom. A parade starts the three-day event. A $50 prize is given to the adult and child who individually find the biggest mushroom; the biggest on record weighed in at 18 ounces. Vendors sell mushrooms in great quantities, and crafters pride themselves with hand-carved wooden mushrooms.

It's not spring in Richmond, Missouri, until you meet your neighbors in the woods on the first mushroom hunt. Secret hunting spots are not often shared, but all share the celebration of the mushrooms.

Submitted by Jerry McCarter, Richmond, Missouri

94. The Secret of Missouri's Dinosaurs

In 1942, geologist Dan Stewart discovered what Missourians thought were cow bones in Bollinger County hills. The Smithsonian Institution purchased what were discovered to be dinosaur bones, but interest waned until the 1970s. Another geologist decided to purchase the dig property and let his paleontologist friend, Guy Darrough, dig the site.

Some fossils were found, such as the *Hypsibema missouriensis* from a duckbilled dinosaur that stretched about 25 feet in length, had 1,000 teeth and weighed as much as an elephant. The species was designated Missouri's official state dinosaur in 2004. If these fossils and bones had not been packed in clay, they would have turned to dust millions of years ago.

Now Mr. Darrough makes a living from his passion. He created Lost World Studios in Arnold, Missouri, where he creates life-size models of dinosaurs for display in museums and exhibits around the world. Learn more by e-mailing to info@lostworldstudios.com or calling 636-282-0970. Visit the Web site at www.lostworldstudios.com.

Submitted by Guy Darrough, Arnold, Missouri

95. The Secrets of Moberly, Missouri

On September 27, 1866, the largest city in Randolph County was born. The magical overnight development of Moberly, Missouri, actually was the product of a railroad auction. The North Missouri Railroad Company connected the Charleton and Randolph Railroad at Moberly, as well as the Wabash Railroad shops, and turned the prairie town into a blossoming community, labeled the Magic City.

This railroad town is also in the county of "great divide." It contains a high ridge of land that stretches from Boone County to Iowa and is easily noticed as one travels through the scenic countryside. Water that falls on the eastern slopes of this divide drains into the Mississippi River, while the water falling on the western slopes flows into the Missouri River. Moberly sits on the high point of the divide.

Discover even more "magic" in this quaint community by visiting www.moberlymo.org or calling 660-263-6070.

Submitted by Kristina Finney, Moberly, Missouri

96. The Secret of Missouri's Pecans

Missouri's pecans have a unique taste because of the state's cooler climate and shorter growing season than in the South, typically from April or May to September or October. Five Missouri pecan growers wanted to segregate the Missouri pecan from the dryer southern pecan by creating the Missouri Northern Pecan Growers, L.L.C. From whole, in-shell pecans and fancy pecan pieces to USDA certified 100% organic pecans, you'll enjoy these flavorful nuts for snacking or baking.

In Nevada, Missouri, the pecan growers' products are sold on Hwy. 71 North at 3400 Industrial Parkway. You also can arrange to watch the whole-nut processing by calling ahead to 417-667-3501.

In Brunswick, Missouri, the James Pecan Farms patented the Starking Hardy Giant Pecan. The farm boasts 10,000 pecan trees. In 1982, they built a concrete replica of a nut weighing 12,000 lbs. and measuring 7 by 12 feet that is visible on the north side of Rt. 24. The Brunswick Pecan Festival is held every October. Call 660-548-3427 for more information. To find out about placing nuts from Missouri trees on your table, go to www.mopecans.com.

April is National Pecan Month............crack one up!

Submitted by Charlene Winfiel, Nevada, Missouri

97. The Secret of Centralia, Missouri

The "living legend" of A. Bishop Chance of the A.B. Chance Company is blooming and growing in a privately owned garden, provided by the generosity of the Chance Foundation.

The Chance Gardens surround the 1904 estate, where the Chance family lived from 1954 to 1973. Mr. Chance was influenced by the international gardens he visited, so in 1936 he created his horticultural dream.

More than 300 tons of Missouri stone were used in its original construction, as well as more than 700 varieties of plants and flowers. A rose garden of 400 varieties and a stone arch are the garden's landmark. A wishing well and a grotto are lined with unusual specimens from Missouri's caves.

Mr. Chance's appreciation of Missouri's geological wonders is beautifully displayed in a garden that he envisioned as a delight for many generations.

Tours can be arranged by calling 573-682-5513.

Submitted by Jim Lea, Centralia, Missouri

98. The Secrets of Weston, Missouri

Weston, Missouri, has many secrets because of its early 1830s history along the Missouri River. Just 8 years after the boomtown was established, the Saint George Hotel opened to accommodate steamboat travelers from all walks of life. Weston became one of the two largest ports on the Missouri River, second only to St. Louis.

Surviving three fires, the Saint George Hotel has remained a charming part of Weston's historic ambience for travelers. The 26-room hotel features the latest popular amenities that modern tourists love today.

A unique secret to the hotel is its wine bank, located in the old bank section of the hotel, which serves as the private wine vault. It offers casual seating where you can enjoy a glass of wine from the collection and nightly cocktail nibbles. On occasion, a small stage can provide acoustical performances.

This is a visit you can bank on, right in the heart of Weston. Call 816-640-9902 or visit the Web site at www.thesaintgeorge.com.

Submitted by Sheena Clemons, Weston, Missouri

99. The Secret of the Governor's Mansion

Thousands of tourists visit the Missouri Governor's Mansion each year. Its beauty and charm radiate as each First Lady makes it her home.

One does not have to enter the Victorian mansion to capture the beauty of one of its historic features. The Missouri's Children's Fountain was placed in the mansion's front yard by Maggie Stephens, wife of Governor Lou V. Stephens, in 1900. The cast-iron fountain features cranes. As the years passed, the fountain's structure and function deteriorated into an elaborate flowerbed.

When the mansion celebrated its 125th year, First Lady Jean Carnahan decided to refurbish the fountain. Mrs. Carnahan decided to design and dedicate the fountain to the children of the mansion. The 9-year-old girl depicted in the fountain is Carrie Crittenden, daughter of Governor and Mrs. T.T. Crittenden, who died of diphtheria while living in the mansion. She represents "children's health." First Lady Agnes Hadley mentioned the "colored boy, living in the barn behind the mansion." He represents "opportunity." "Today's child" was modeled after Mrs. Carnahan's 5-year-old grandson, Austin Carnahan. Sculptor Jamie Anderson created the intricate detail.

The next time you drive or walk by the mansion, take time to reflect on "Missouri's Children." The fountain is located at 115 Jefferson Street. Call 573-751-7929 for more information.

Submitted by Mary Pat Abele, Boonville, Missouri

100. *The Secret of El Dorado Springs, Missouri*

In 1881, Nathaniel and Waldo Cruce founded El Dorado Springs to accommodate the influx of people coming to drink the "healing water" coming from a natural spring located in the area.

In the beautiful hillside park surrounding the springs, eight young men, under the leadership of C.V. Mickey, started a band in 1886 that is still in existence today. In 1887, their first bandstand was constructed in a two-story style. Then, in 1905, a hexagonal bandstand was erected that then was changed in 1938 to the present bandstand, which is round with a stone foundation.

Band members, once paid only by donations, are now funded by the city of El Dorado Springs. The charter members of the band were great musicians who played many of the old circus marches and overtures that are still played today.

Every summer and weekend, you can hear them play in the scenic park as you rest on the nearby benches. And so the band plays on!

For their latest schedule, call the Chamber of El Dorado Springs at 417-876-4154.

Submitted by Lillian Sunderwirth, El Dorado Springs, Missouri

the Secrets
and their Regions

Kansas City Region

Springfield Region

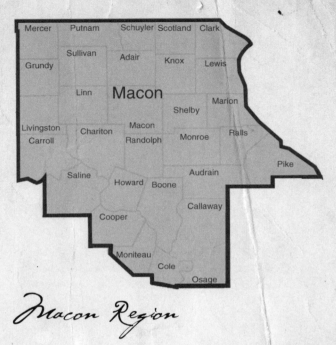

Macon Region

Lincoln

Montgomery

Warren St. Charles

St. Louis

Gasconade

Franklin St. Louis

St. Louis

Jefferson

St. Louis Region

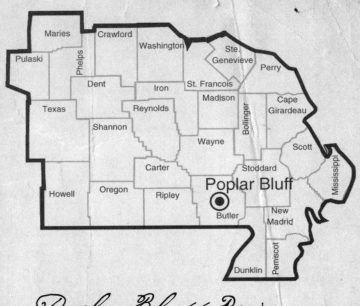

Poplar Bluff Region

All Regions

Index of Missouri Secrets

Mushroom Festival	93	EVENT
National Park Academy of the Arts	69	ARTS
National Shrine of St. Mary	2	SEE
Old Peace Chapel	23	SEE
Old Tyme Apple Festival	66	EVENT
Patricia's Tearoom	39	DINING
Phythian Castle	51	SEE
Pirtle Winery	59	WINE
Pony Express Museum	44	SPECIALTY MUSEUM
Pumpkin Festival	53	EVENT
Rafter P. Ranch Historic Home	87	HISTORIC SITE
River of Life Farm	80	LODGING, WEEKEND GETAWAY
Route 66 Drive-In	76	HISTORIC SITE, MOVIE THEATRE
Saint Ambrose Church	55	SEE
Saint George Hotel	98	LODGING
Saxon Memorial	61	HISTORIC SITE
Show-Me-Missouri Fish Mobile Aquarium	57	SEE
Soybean Festival	7	EVENT
Taille de Noyer home	75	HISTORIC SITE
Thespian Hall	25	SEE
Tower Rock Winery	61	WINE
Trailhead Brewing Company	84	DINING, BREWERY
Wenwood Farm Winery	59	WINE
Westminster College	3	HISTORIC SITE
White Rose Winery	59	WINE
Wib's BBQ	17	DINING
Wine Country Garden & Nursery	40	SPECIALTY SHOPPING
Yates House Bed & Breakfast	22	LODGING
Zachariah Foss House	59	LODGING

Index of Missouri Names

100 BEST KEPT SECRETS OF *Missouri*

Index of Missouri Towns & Cities

Photo Credits

Page 3, 8, 11,12, 13, 14, 16, 23, 25, 27, 46, 47, 51, 79, 85, 89, 99, 100, courtesy of Ann Hazelwood

Page 6, courtesy of Perry County Republic Monitor, Perry, Missouri

Page 20, 34, 35, 36, 40, 42, 48, 53, 56, 65, 88, courtesy of the West End Word

Page 19, courtesy of Cuba Chamber of Commerce

Page 30, courtesy of Cape Girardeau Convention & Visitors Center

Page 63, courtesy Leila Cahoon

Page 67, photo by Larry Duffy, courtesy of Whittaker Homes

Page 71, courtesy of Nelson Weber

Page 73, courtesy of Luxenhaus Farm, Marthasville, Mo

Page 75, courtesy of Taille del Noyer House

Page 77, courtesy of Jan Lewien

Page 94, photo by Guy Darrough

Page 97, courtesy of the Chance Foundation

Page 100, courtesy Lillian Sunderwirth

Maps pp. 101 – 106, courtesy of Missouri Department of Natural Resources

About the Author

Ann M. Hazelwood is a Missouri native, born in Perryville, Missouri. Her adult life brought her to St. Charles, Missouri, where she raised her family and started a business called Patches etc. in 1979. She is nationally known as a quilt shop owner, quilt appraiser and author for the American Quilting Society. She also serves on the Board of the Museum of the American Quilting Society in Paducah, Kentucky. She has been honored with many awards for her entrepreneurial efforts, such as "Retailer of the Year" for the city of St. Charles, Missouri.

She is married to Keith Hazelwood, a local attorney in St. Charles, and has two sons, Joel and Jason Watkins, and two stepsons, Rocky and Robert Hazelwood.

The St. Charles community has been near and dear to her heart. In 2005, Ann wrote *100 Things to Do In and Around St. Charles.* She is active in many organizations and has served as President of many, including the St. Charles Chamber of Commerce.

In Ann's daily activities, she is an avid promoter of tourism. She visits not only with Missourians on a daily basis, but visitors from all over the world. She is proud of her home state of Missouri, and the diversity that the state has to offer in its communities, neighborhoods and tourist attractions. She feels there are many wonderful secrets to share in this "Show Me" state. With the help of her contributors, she chose 100 secrets to share with you.